Hope hope you enjoy the
book. Erma

I'm Nobody

My Mother Said It;
I No Longer Believe It

ERMA STEPPE

iUniverse, Inc.
Bloomington

I'm Nobody
My Mother Said It; I No Longer Believe It

iUniverse books may be ordered through booksellers or by contacting:

iUniverse
1663 Liberty Drive
Bloomington, IN 47403
www.iuniverse.com
1-800-Authors (1-800-288-4677)

Because of the dynamic nature of the Internet, any Web addresses or links contained in this book may have changed since publication and may no longer be valid. The views expressed in this work are solely those of the author and do not necessarily reflect the views of the publisher, and the publisher hereby disclaims any responsibility for them.

ISBN: 978-1-4502-7398-5 (pbk)
ISBN: 978-1-4502-7399-2 (cloth)
ISBN: 978-1-4502-7400-5 (ebk)

Library of Congress Control Number: 2010916923

Printed in the United States of America

iUniverse rev. date: 1/26/2011

To Susie Donahue, whose help and support carried me through the emotional difficulty of writing this book.

CONTENTS

Introduction   ix

1. My First Memories   1

2. Safety Do's and Don'ts   10

3. Guardian Angel   17

4. The Difficulties of Learning   23

5. My Tattoo and My Barbara   30

6. Alone, Hungry, and Scared   34

7. Mom's Arrest—My Fault   40

8. My Family of Sticks   45

9. Nobody Tells   48

10. Only One … Me   54

11. Foster Care—Eyes Wide Open   60

12. My Plan In Motion   63

13. Reunited and Moving   70

14. Frank, Another Guardian Angel   74

15. Married Life—Who Knew?   79

16. Bellefontaine—Responsibilities and Missionaries   95

17. The Mormon Church—A New Way of Life   106

18. Buckhorn and Reviving the Past   116

19. Bath County—Family Life   121

20. Divorce—Who Knew   127

21. Endings and Beginnings   134

Epilogue   161

INTRODUCTION

At the age of sixty-four, I still have mixed feelings about my life. There's a part of me that thinks time is running out and I want to do things; I want to live. Then there's a part of me that wants to sit and watch—not to be seen or heard, to just watch.

These have always been my feelings. The part of me that wants to live has grown stronger, but the other part of me still flinches when faced with even the smallest thing that can hurt me emotionally or physically. If I had to choose between the two, I would choose physical harm. I've always gotten over physical pain faster.

When I was sixteen years old, my mother said to me, "You are nobody. You don't count. The only ones that count are me and this baby."

I stood there in the one-room rented apartment over a bar on Main Street in Columbus, Ohio. I just stood there while she screamed at me. I didn't say anything. I felt so little and afraid. I wanted to go back—but back where? *I remember thinking, I can't take my body, so I'll just go in my head.* But I couldn't. I couldn't get to my safe place for some reason. I couldn't find my safe spot.

I had taken a chance, another chance, and then a big risk. I had given up all my safe places to be there with my mother. I had given up everything and everyone who had always come to my rescue before. I ran away from the Pomeroy Children's Home. Barbara had released me from state custody. I ran to find my mother. I gave up everything to find her and be with her.

I knew that I could drop off the face of the earth and no one would question my whereabouts. I would not be missed. No one would come looking for me. No one would ever ask, "Where is Erma?" This was the first time I was ever truly alone with nowhere to go and no one to come and get me. I was sixteen years old, and my mother had tossed me out of her one-room apartment. I had nothing and no one to fall back on for support.

I had no money and no clothes except for what I was wearing. I had not eaten in two days. My mother was drunk and angry. She had always been a mean drunk. In my haste to find my mother, I guess I had forgotten that. She was looking for someone to take her anger out on. That someone was me. It had always been me.

It was so different from what I had dreamed about all those years I spent in and out of children's homes and in one foster home after another. All those nights lying awake and dreaming of her taking me in her arms, telling me how much she had missed me and how very much she loved me. We would never be separated again. My mother would keep her little girl safe and always love her. That was my dream.

This was not my dream—not this screaming, angry, mean drunk throwing me out onto the streets of a big city. She stood in front of me spitting and cursing.

My dream never did come true.

Here I am at the age of sixty-four, and a few weeks ago, my mother looked at me and said, "You don't count. You are nobody. The only ones that count are me and my boy. Stay away from me!" I finally realized she was being honest with me. It was very painful for me to accept those hurtful words. She has never loved me. She will never love me. I will never be her little girl.

This time, I got the message. My mother was stone cold sober when she said it; she hasn't had a drink in about twenty years. She looked me straight in the eye and told me she hated me, I was nobody, I didn't count. She never flinched once. The message was loud and clear.

Mom has always seen me as her rival. I was the little girl her male friends looked at with lust. My mother wanted to be the one they lusted after. She did not want me to exist. She had never wanted me.

I am now going to write my life story. I can't put a specific age or date on siblings' births, my birth date, chronological events, school dates, and more because we had no celebrations and there were no mentions of any ages. I didn't know my actual age or last name until I applied for my marriage license. My mom told me she thought my birthday was October 8, 1944 or 1945. A woman at the county clerk's office was more helpful than my mother was.

Maybe this book will help me understand myself. Maybe I can learn to use my strengths, accept my faults, and understand my feelings. Maybe there are other daughters and sons who will understand my story and know they are not alone. I wish for them to find peace in their heart.

Chapter 1
MY FIRST MEMORIES

This is hard for me to write because I can't set an age and I don't have a time frame. One of my first and most vivid memories is that of my toes. They were soft, warm, and wiggly. I liked feeling them; I liked my toes. They gave me joy.

All of my memories at this time were of me on the floor. I remember sitting up. A big person walked by me on my floor. She wanted me to stay out of her way. Sometimes she stepped on my parts. She stepped on my fingers, my wonderful toes, and sometimes on my arms or my legs. I would cry when this happened. My crying made the big person angry. I don't think she purposely stepped on me; I think I was just in her way. There was a place I needed to go to when she was on my floor. I needed to get behind the door. She would forget about me there. Behind that door was my safe place.

I remember she would put things on the floor, and I would put these things in my mouth. I liked that feeling. Sometimes she dropped things, and after she left, I would put whatever they were in my mouth.

I have no memory of anyone else at this time. I had no knowledge of the rest of the house; my floor and my door were my world. I later learned that the floor and the door were in the kitchen. I don't remember a bed unless my bed was in the kitchen, possibly on the floor behind the door. At some point, I realized that there was another me in a different room. This is the first time I truly remember joy. I couldn't get to the other side because of something in the doorway, and I could hear the big person talking to the other me.

She called him Billy. Soon Billy would be on one side of the doorway and I would be on the other side. I could touch Billy. I felt his arm. It felt like mine. We learned to play through the doorway. He was like me, and I felt good and happy about this.

The big person liked Billy too. I could see her picking him up and talking to him. I don't remember any jealousy or bad feelings about this. I loved to watch her with him, and this made him even more special to me.

I remember one time Billy pulled my hair and I bit his arm. That was the first time I remember being slapped. The big person was very mad at me. I remember crying and waking up behind the door.

All I remember after that is happiness. My world was Billy. At some point, we were together in the same room. The chair—what had been between us—was no longer in the doorway. I knew my place was still in the kitchen. My safe place was still behind the door.

I couldn't wait to be with Billy whenever I was awake. We were both walking and running. Billy called the big person Mommy. I called the big person Mommy one time, and she quickly and sternly let me know she was not my mommy. I was to call her Aunt Mary. I'm not sure what age I was. I remember Billy, Aunt Mary, and a dog. I loved to hug and rub the dog.

The next event I remember is a woman and a man coming to the house one night. The woman picked me up and called me Erma. That was the first time I heard my name … Erma. The woman told me she was my mommy and the man was my daddy. She put me in a dress and tried to comb my hair. That hurt.

Aunt Mary and this woman talked for a long, long time. The woman took me to a car, and I cried. I did not want to leave the other me behind. I did not want to leave Billy. We left anyway.

I sat on the woman's lap, and the man drove. They made several stops. They were drinking, and I had lots of things to eat. I found out later that we had driven to Columbus, Ohio.

The man and the woman were mad at each other. They hit and screamed at each other. The man hurt my mommy. I wanted my safe place, but it was at Aunt Mary's. I went under the bed. I did not make a sound. I had learned very early at Aunt Mary's about being quiet and staying out of sight.

The police and a woman came. My mommy and daddy went to jail, and I went to a big place with lots of children. It was my first trip to a children's home. It would not be my last. I'm not sure how long I stayed there—maybe about six weeks.

Mom went to jail for disturbing the peace. She also assaulted another woman. Eventually, Mom got out and came to get me. I remember crying when she took me away, so I must have liked being in the home. I have no memory of my time there.

My mother was Agnes B. She had six brothers, three sisters, and one half-brother from her father's first marriage; there were eleven children in the B. family. The family was extremely poor. My grandfather never owned or rented a home. He just found an empty house and moved in, making it his new home. He was a squatter. Very few ever questioned or messed with him and his six sons. They had a reputation for taking and keeping what they wanted.

Mom has said many times that Aunt Mary was her favorite sibling. Mom dominated her sister and often bragged about holding Aunt Mary until the school bus passed so they didn't have to go to school. Aunt Mary liked going to school, but Mom dictated what they did. Mom controlled Aunt Mary most of their lives.

Mom also ruled at home. She had violent temper tantrums when she didn't get her way. Mom's mother also felt dominated by her wants and demands. During one of these violent incidents, Mom's dad sent her away from home with a gun pointed at her head. Grandpa Fred was the only family member to stand up to Mom.

Agnes left her home at the age of eighteen. She went to live with her sister, Mary, and her husband, Howard. She became pregnant with me shortly after she moved in with Aunt Mary. Mom was pregnant by her sister's husband, Howard. Mom always had a way of getting in and getting what she wanted. No one ever stood in her way. I was born on October 8, 1944, at the old White Cross Hospital in Columbus, Ohio.

Mom had hitchhiked often, and during one of those adventures, she met a man she really liked and had sex with him during the ride. She gave me his last name, Morgan.

As I look back now, I can honestly state that my mom has never cared about me. She didn't care about me as I was growing up, and she certainly doesn't now as I write my story at the age of sixty-four.

Agnes was a beautiful woman. She was not thin or petite; she was built, and she exuded sexuality. Mom was all woman. She had beautiful green eyes. Her complexion was dark, and she had dark brown hair. She stood about five foot nine.

Once Agnes began dating, she took excellent care of her appearance. She washed and curled her hair daily. She took care of her nails and kept them polished. She used makeup, especially if a male was going to be in her sights. She always wore hose and dressed nicely. She knew how to take care of herself. Even now at the age of eighty-four, she has her hair curled, nails done, and bright red lipstick on.

Agnes has always been different whenever a man is in the picture. Even now, she uses what she perceives as a little girl's voice to attract these men. She talks baby talk and will sing and dance for and with these men. She wears bows, ribbons, and flowers in her hair. Most of her life she wore dresses. Only in the last ten years has she begun wearing pants.

Agnes is an alcoholic. She began her drinking career as a child sneaking booze with her sister, Mary, at her father's still. This was at least a weekly event. I can remember sitting around the table with other family members and Mom and Aunt Mary telling stories about their trips to the still. They often talked about getting caught by Grandpa, and how angry he would be at them. They also giggled when their brothers got blamed for the missing brew.

Mom spent all her life chasing after men. Her taste in men is unique. It has never mattered to her who they are, what they look like, how they smell, or what they do. Her requirements were that they be sexually active, drink and supply her with booze, and they must like to brawl. Consequently, she always ended up with men who used her to get what they wanted and then took what they really wanted—her little girl, her daughter. Mom didn't know or care because she was usually passed out or moving on to the next man.

Mom's children always suffered from her good times and her male friends. She demanded to be the center of attention, and she wanted all men to want her. She wanted to be a cute little girl and would do anything to keep her man. She would abandon her home and her children just to be with a man, any man. Mom did not suffer any consequences or feelings of guilt for her behavior, except for the occasional pregnancy.

Mom has told me several times she has no regrets for enjoying her life. She said that a person should have a good time. I just looked at her and thought, *what about us?*

Mom and I went back to Aunt Mary's. This is the first time I remember seeing Billy's father and Aunt Mary's husband, Howard. We all called him Pap. I remember I liked being around Pap. He didn't pick me up or talk to me, but I liked him. Mom did not have a man with her, and I always had a wonderful time when she didn't have a man. Billy and I played together and had candy and plenty of food to eat. Mom and Aunt Mary would get falling-down drunk every day. During this time, Aunt Mary seemed to like me a little.

One of the most powerful and memorable events took place while we were all together having fun. We had a wood-burning stove. At the bottom of the stove was a shaker used to shake hot ashes down into a pan. On this night, someone had left the shaker sticking out at the bottom. Billy went over and shook it, and hot embers fell into the pan. Just as the hot embers fell, Billy fell—face and hands into the pan. We were very small, maybe two or three years old at the time. Billy was screaming, and I remember the burning pain. It was unbearable. I knew we were really hurt. We screamed and cried all night. As the years passed, I believed I was the one injured on that night. I remember the burning and the tears.

In August 2009, Billy and I were discussing this event and he showed me his scars. I was astonished. Billy was the one who had gotten burned that night, not me. The pain that I felt was a searing burning pain, but it was Billy's pain I was feeling, because at the time Billy and I were one.

Mom went away again, and I was left with Billy, Pap, and Aunt Mary. I remember being happy. I didn't have a bed to sleep in at night, and I don't remember getting ready for bed. I remember waking on the floor, on a chair, or sometimes on the couch. I slept in the clothes I wore during the day. I remember it being very cold outside, so it must have been winter. I got sick. I hurt everywhere.

Aunt Mary got someone to take us to the hospital, and the people at the hospital put me in a bed. They put a big see-through bag all over me. This was my first time in a bed and I liked it. It seemed like I was there for a long time.

I wouldn't talk to anyone. I found out early that not talking worked best for me. The people at the hospital called me Baby Jane. I'm not sure if Aunt Mary gave them my name or if she could even pronounce my name. I remember people asking me questions. They wanted to know my name, where I lived, and who brought me to the hospital. I didn't talk.

Finally, two women came to the hospital and got me. They took me to the big house with all the children, the Children's Home in Columbus, Ohio. Days or weeks later, Mom came to get me. I did not want to go. I did not know her.

I was later told by Mom that Aunt Mary had taken me to the hospital and left me there. Aunt Mary didn't tell the people at the hospital anything about me. She just dropped me off and left. Eventually Mom came back to Aunt Mary's. Aunt Mary told her what she had done and where I was, so Mom came and got me. It was just Mom and me, and we went back to Aunt Mary's.

Mom and I slept in a bed at Aunt Mary's. This was my first time I remember sleeping with my mother. I remember Mom smelled so good and was so warm. I snuggled, feeling so safe and warm in her arms. I felt loved. I still had not spoken since Aunt Mary had taken me to the hospital.

A man named Bill came to Aunt Mary's looking for Mom. She and I left with him. I still was not talking to anyone. My plan was to get Mom to pick me up, hold me, and talk to me the way Aunt Mary talked to Billy. I don't remember missing Billy or anyone else because I was with my mom.

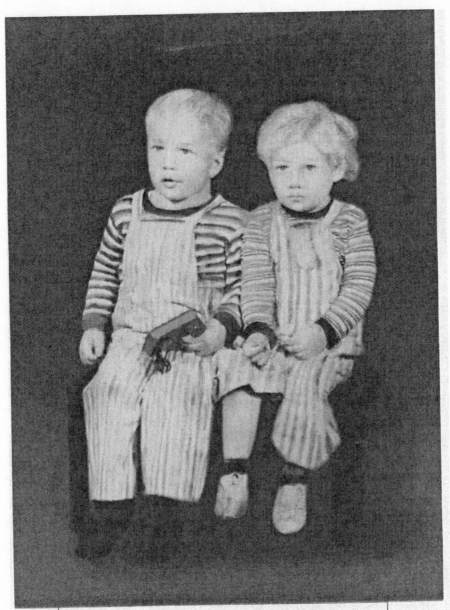

(Above) *Me and Billy Donahue. Mom and my Aunt Mary took us to the Meigs County Fair where a photographer took our picture. This is the only picture I have of my childhood.*

MY MOM

20s   30s

40s

Agnes Bachus at 60 years

Doc. 1

3-41-1   THE COLUMBUS BLANK BOOK MFG. CO., COL., O.   3757

JOURNAL ENTRY---Order for Citation
Gen'l Code. Sec. 1648

Juvenile Court, *Franklin* County, Ohio
May 12, 19 *47*.

In the Matter of
Erma Older _____

neglected
an alleged dependent minor.

This day *C. R. Rivert* filed with the Judge of this
Court an affidavit setting forth that *Erma Older*
a minor under the age of eighteen years, appears to be *neglected dependent*
It is therefore ordered that a citation issue requiring such minor
to appear, and *Agnes and Bill Older* the persons having custody
or control of the child or with whom it may be, to appear with said
minor before the Judge of this Court, on the *15th* day of
May , 19 *47* , at *9:00* o'clock *A* M., and this
cause is continued.

_____
Judge

1. Dependent, Neglected or Delinquent

Child taken into custody and lodged at Franklin Co. Home.
Parents arrested for drunk and disorderly, disturbing the
peace, destruction of property.
Mrs. Older also arrested for assault on police officer
and Social worker.

Chapter 2
SAFETY DO'S AND DON'TS

My world had taken on an entirely new concept—survival. To survive was my priority. Avoiding getting hurt was on my mind both day and night. This was my thought every minute of every hour.

If you have ever lived with one or two mean alcoholics, you know what I'm talking about. Sometimes they would focus on each other. Fighting, throwing things, cursing, and threatening to kill each other was their way of life. I remember blood, black eyes, and broken glass. They did this day and night until they passed out or the police came, and then they would stop fighting for a while. I liked it best when the police came.

Living with alcoholics, you learn that it is their nature to prey and focus on the weakest. The weakest was me, and I suffered greatly when they focused on me. I cried from their cruelty. They hurt me physically, mentally, and emotionally.

The problem with being a child in this situation is that *you can't win.* They keep working on you until you're broken and crying. Should you not break, they will continue until you lose. They want someone to pay. I wonder if anyone knows why someone must pay. When you lose, they feel satisfied. It makes them feel important.

I believe I was about four or five years old when Baby Freddie came to live with us. Freddie was named after my grandpa, my mom's dad. It's so strange because I know he was there, but I don't remember anything about him. I don't remember him crying, Mom feeding him, a diaper being changed, or him ever being held by anyone. Now there were four of us living in a one-room apartment over a bar in Columbus, Ohio: Bill, Mom, Freddie, and me.

This is the first time I remember being sexually messed with by Bill. He was mean to me, and whenever Mom was around, he did not speak to me. As time went on, Bill became much more sexual with me. I'm not going to go into these specifics because it was not so much the things he did to me or the things he had me do, it was how he made me feel inside. He made me feel afraid, ashamed, dirty, and ugly. I was and felt helpless. Before the sexual abuse began, I was able to have some small pleasures as a child. After he began the abuse, I felt like an old can, rusty and dirty with nothing inside me. I remember thinking that if Mommy found out she would hate me, beat me, and probably put me on the streets to live. She would lock me outside.

The main thing I have learned about pedophiles is they make sure the coast is clear before the abuse starts. I've been the victim of several, and their main goal is not to get caught.

I don't remember thinking about anything or anyone but me. I needed to have food to eat and not get hurt. If I did get hurt, I needed to know how to make it better, know how to avoid Mom and Bill, and how to stay very quiet. I do remember thinking, *I get hurt by big people, but I also need big people to be okay.* I don't remember wanting to go back to Aunt Mary's, but I do remember thinking I wanted to go back to the Big House. I really wanted the police to come, but I was sure they would know what was going on and they would hate me.

I can't seem to put all my emotions on paper. There are so many different ones. Sexual abuse is the death of a child. It rips out what makes you want to be close to other people. It steals a person's life because there's never a normal life after sexual abuse. It never goes away; it remains in the crevices of your mind.

I know there are different types of sexual abuse. Mine had nothing to do with me as a person. I was merely an object to be used for someone's amusement and pleasure—no love, no warmth, just an object, an empty can.

Aunt Mary and Billy entered into my life again. Aunt Mary looked like your typical German woman. She stood about four foot ten. Her complexion was dark, and her hair and her eyes were black. She was noticeably uneducated.

She had only attended the second or third grade of school, occasionally. She had a dark, menacing look about her, and I knew without being told not to cross Aunt Mary. Although she could be sweet at times, it was like there was a battle going on inside of her not to lash out. She had a violent temper and could explode instantly. Anyone or anything in her path was in immediate danger of being destroyed or seriously harmed.

The only person I ever knew to stand up against Aunt Mary was Mom. Aunt Mary was the older of the two. I'm not sure what it was that gave Mom power over Aunt Mary. Mom may have been smarter and was certainly a bigger, taller woman, but I don't believe that had anything to do with their relationship. Mom had bullied her entire family all of her life.

As far as I know, no one has ever heard Aunt Mary question Agnes about her having sex and producing a child with Aunt Mary's husband. I believe Agnes could do no wrong in Aunt Mary's eyes.

Mom had sex with her sister's husband and gave birth to their child only six months after Aunt Mary gave birth to her and Howard's son, Billy. I was the result of Mom and Pap's affair. I believe this is why Aunt Mary treated me so poorly. Aunt Mary blamed me, not Mom. My mother left me for months at a time with her sister who she knew hated me and would treat me accordingly.

I guess going to town with Mom gave Aunt Mary things she had only dreamed of, such as men, drinks, romance, and sex. And in town, she could dance. Mom was worldlier than Aunt Mary, and I think Aunt Mary saw Mom's world as glamorous when they were together.

During Mom's incarcerations, she learned how to bathe herself, wash and curl her hair, apply makeup, and use deodorants and perfumes. Aunt Mary did not have these skills.

I never really did understand Mom and Aunt Mary's feelings for each other. They always rescued each other when one of them was in need or danger. I do believe they truly loved each other. I also believe they both hated me. I believe that they hated other females, especially their own daughters.

The life that Mom dragged me through and the way she has treated me my entire life proves this to me. I have also seen Aunt Mary commit similar violations against her only daughter. I guess the best way to explain it is to say they were both cruel and dangerous women. Aunt Mary just hid her actions better than Mom did. Aunt Mary was not in the public eye as much as Mom, so she stayed under the police and social workers' radar. Also, you must remember, children don't tell.

Another man began living with Mom and Bill. He was a friend of Bill's from the junk yard where they both worked. The man's name was Dick.

One day, Mom told me to get in the car. She said we were going to go get Aunt Mary. Bill drove from Columbus to Galena, Ohio. It was dark when we arrived at Aunt Mary's. As soon as we got there, I jumped out of the car and ran past Mom to get in the house to see Billy. Bill, Dick, and my little brother Freddie stayed in the car. Aunt Mary had her bags packed and was ready to go with us to Columbus.

We started out the door when Pap came in the house. Pap said Aunt Mary wasn't taking Billy anywhere. I remember hearing a loud fight with lots of cursing and screaming. I could hear Mom over everyone and I knew to stay out of the way. Pap told Aunt Mary to get out but leave Billy. Aunt Mary began to back down, but Mom wasn't backing down for anyone. Mom told Aunt Mary and Billy to go to the car.

Pap was no match for Mom. I knew to get out of Mom's way. I got behind an old rocking chair and watched from behind it. Aunt Mary started out the door with Billy, and Pap turned to take Billy. I saw Mom reach over to the ironing board where Aunt Mary had been ironing. She grabbed the flat iron and hit Pap over the head. He went to the floor, and blood started pouring from his head. I just knew Pap was dead.

Mom told me to go to the car. Billy and Aunt Mary were still standing by the door. Billy and I were crying, afraid to say anything. Mom got in the front seat with Bill, Dick, and Freddie. Aunt Mary, Billy, and I sat in the back seat. Everyone was quiet for a long time. The only sound was Billy and me sniffling.

Pap didn't die, but he was in the hospital for weeks.

When Pap regained consciousness, he started walking down the road. He was going to Letart Falls because he thought that was where Aunt Mary had gone with Billy.

Pap fainted along the road and was taken to the hospital. He had no identification on him. He was in the hospital for some time and had a metal plate put in the back of his head.

A neighbor of Pap's heard the ruckus, saw Bill's car leaving, and went into the house. She saw all the blood where Pap's head had bled so much and called the police. The police began looking for Mom and Aunt Mary for possible murder charges.

We arrived at Mom's one-room apartment late that night. The next day, Aunt Mary and Billy moved into a one-room apartment down the hall from us, over the bar on Main Street. Dick moved in with Aunt Mary and Billy. We always seemed to have food and money. We had a lot of car parts in our room, and Bill and Dick would work on the parts, load them in our car, and sell them.

I had a good time playing with Billy, and I remember this as a very happy time in my life. I remember looking at cars on the street and seeing people walking on the sidewalks. I think this was the first time I realized the world was moving and people were busy. I had Billy; we were talking and playing and we had food to eat. Mom seemed happy.

Our happiness came to an abrupt end. The police came one night and woke everyone. They came to our room and then went to Aunt Mary's room. All the adults were arrested on possible murder charges, and the police saw all the stolen auto parts in the room when they came to get Mom and Aunt Mary.

The police stayed until two women came to our rooms. They put Freddie, Billy, and me in a car and took us to a children's home in Columbus, Ohio.

Bill and Mom went before the judge and were given a year in prison for stealing and selling stolen property. Freddie and I had to stay in the Franklin County Children's Home while they did their jail time.

I never saw Freddie while we were in the home. I did get to see Billy at playtime once a day. Billy and I sat in the playroom and played with trucks every day. I could hardly wait for playtime so I could see him. The playroom was in the basement of the home, and we found out that if you had something to stand on, you could look out the basement windows.

Pap showed up a few weeks after the arrests. The judge let Aunt Mary and Billy go home with Pap. Nobody knew that Pap was my dad—at least no one was telling. I didn't even know he was my dad at the time. I just knew he was my Pap.

Billy and I were in the playroom when a woman came and said that Billy's dad had come to take him home. I got up to go with Billy, and the woman said no, not me, just Billy. I said, "But he's my Pap too." She said only Billy could go.

She took Billy, and I was alone again. Billy had promised me he would tell Pap I was there too and they would come in and get me. I waited and ran to look out the window. I could see Billy and Pap walking away. Pap was holding Billy's hand. Billy kept trying to turn around, but Pap kept him walking away from me.

Years later, I remember thinking about my Pap and the day he came to take Billy home. Pap was a tall, thin, quiet man. He stood about six foot two. He had piercing, pale blue eyes. His skin was so pale, it was almost transparent. His hair was the color of light orange, almost the color of shiny gold. He was balding. I rarely heard him speak, and when he did, it was in a soft tone. Pap would stutter when he got excited or when he was drinking.

I remember that he drank often and kept a bottle hidden wherever he lived. He was not a mean drunk. Usually he would just go to sleep unless someone was picking on him. Pap was a peaceful alcoholic. I can't ever remember seeing him angry. He wore bib overalls all the time; I can't remember seeing him in anything else.

I don't know and no one will ever be able to tell me, but I truly believe that Pap loved both Aunt Mary and Mom. I believe with all my heart that he loved me and always accepted me as his child.

That was my Pap walking away with Billy because he couldn't prove I was his child. He couldn't take me with him and Billy. There have never been any records to prove this well-known family fact.

That was my Pap and my Billy walking away.

I remember thinking that my tears were salty. I never played with the trucks the rest of my time there. I quit talking. I just stood at the window hoping Billy would come back. He did not. I found out later that Billy was there for six weeks and I was there for a year.

Every Sunday afternoon after church, all the children would gather in the big sitting room. People came to see some of the children. No one ever came to see me.

I must have been five or six years of age because I don't recall being in school. On Sundays, I went to Sunday school and then we would have lunch. This was the home's regular Sunday schedule. I'm not sure where Freddie was all this time. I had not seen Freddie since our arrival. No one ever talked about him, and I wasn't talking to anyone anymore.

Doc. 2

3-41-1   THE COLUMBUS BLANK BOOK MFG. CO., COL., O.   3757

JOURNAL ENTRY---Order for Citation
Gen'l Code, Sec. 1648

Juvenile Court, _Franklin_ County, Ohio

November 4, 19_50_.

In the Matter of
Erma Older and Freddie Older an alleged ~~neglected~~ *dependent* minor.s

This day _Robie Hudson_ filed *with the Judge of this*
Court an affidavit setting forth that _Erma and Freddie Older_
a minor[2] *under the age of eighteen years, appears to be* : _neglected and_ *dependent*
    It is therefore ordered that a citation issue requiring such minor
to appear, and _Jaye and Bill Older_ *the persons having custody*
or control of the child or with whom it may be, to appear with said
minor before the Judge of this Court, on the _6th_ *day of*
November, *19* _50_, *at* _9:00_ *o'clock* _A_ *M., and this*
cause is continued.

_____
Judge

1. Dependent, Neglected or Delinquent

Erma and Freddie were removed from parents and
taken to the ~~Franklin~~ Co. Children's Home, Columbus O.

Chapter 3
GUARDIAN ANGEL

Something happened while I was standing looking out that basement window. Some would say it was just a child's imagination, and others would say it was utter nonsense. According to me and maybe a few others, it was my guardian angel. The trees were blowing, and I think they were pine trees because the branches were so low.

This wonderful figure in all white came out toward me as the branches parted. It did not appear to be a woman or a man. I believed if I blew on it, it would have floated up to the clouds. Touching it would have turned it to a pool of white water.

I still was not talking to anyone. The figure before me knew my questions and thoughts.

I thought, *who are you?*

The figure replied, "I am going to stay with you."

Why? I thought.

The figure said, "Father wants me to live with you. You cannot live without me. I can live in your heart. Others will not see me."

Will I always be able to see you?

"No, but I will always be there."

How will I know you're always with me?

"You will feel me."

Will you be in front of me?

"No, beside you."

What side?

"You know where your heart is?"

Yes. I put my right hand on my heart the way we did when we said the Pledge of Allegiance each morning. *Why are you staying with me? I am so bad.*

"No, you are God's child." The figure seemed to float toward me to my left side, and I never saw it again.

At the children's home, I had been going to church for the first time in my life. They talked about God. My vision may have been my imagination or it may have been a dream, but I do know I was never alone again. I know it was and is my guardian angel.

I changed after that—things changed. I seemed stronger. I started praying like they did in Sunday school. I had answers come to mind as soon as I needed them. Sometimes in my weakest moments, I felt my strongest. My guardian angel was my guide. It was the first time I realized I had two worlds. I could leave one and enter the other and have a good life. My imagination became my safety outlet.

All the children were sitting in the waiting room where people came to see them. A woman walked in, and my mom was with her. Mom didn't say anything to me. The woman said I was going home. Mom wanted to know where my clothes were. I didn't say anything. Mom asked, "Has the cat still got your tongue?" The woman told Mom she would go and get my clothes.

So I left with Mom. I was happy to see her, but I was sad to be leaving the home. Mom and I went up another floor and picked up Freddie. He had been there the whole time, and no one had let me see or talk to him. Freddie was walking and talking. I remember he cried because he did not want to leave the home and go with us. We walked down the street and got in a car. Mom was with Bill again. I don't know how, but they had money. They stopped several times and went into bars.

Freddie and I were left in the car while they stayed inside the bars. I remember it getting very dark and I fell asleep. I remember waking and seeing that Mom and Bill were in the front seat asleep. I had to pee. I was afraid to wake Mom up, so I went in my underwear. Mom was upset and said I should have awakened her instead of wetting myself like a little baby.

Bill drove to a store and got some coffee, some bread, and bologna. It tasted so good. We drove a long time and ended up somewhere on the Ohio River. We stopped there for the night. It was like camping, and we stayed there all night. I learned at a very young age that alcoholics always have alcohol and cigarettes. Freddie and I had bologna.

The next morning, we washed in the river. Bill drove to a store, and he and Mom got coffee. Bill also got Freddie and me a little cake and a pop.

Bill drove to Grandma's house. This was the second time I had seen my grandmother. Grandmother came to the door and told Mom she could not stay there with that man and those kids. She said Grandpa had died and Woodrow was taking care of her. She wanted us to go away.

I remember thinking my grandma looked very strange. Her hair was long, unkempt, and hanging down her back. She was wearing several dresses. There was a scared look about her. Grandma was still talking, and Mom was acting like Grandma wasn't saying anything.

Bill got Freddie and me out of the car, and Mom told me to take Freddie under a big tree in the front yard. Grandma turned her back to us and continued talking. She seemed to be talking to herself. Mom said, "I'm going in the house to get some food and money to get a place to live." Mom went into the old house and came out with some food. I don't remember what it was she brought out to eat.

I knew something was very wrong with Grandma. Why would she let Mom push her way around in the house and take her food and money? While I was sitting under the big tree in Grandma's yard, I remembered the first time I saw my grandma. I didn't remember her looking like she did on this day—unkempt and afraid. I remembered Mom, a man, and me going to Grandma and Grandpa's house. Grandpa was sitting under the big tree. He had a block of wood sitting beside him and was cracking nuts with a hammer. He picked me up and put me on his lap and fed me walnuts. They were good. He would crack a nut, take a bite, and then give me a bite. I liked Grandpa. He told me my belly button was where an Indian had shot me with an arrow. Grandpa and I went into the house where Grandma was working. Grandma had the table set with plenty of food. I remembered fried chicken, big biscuits, green beans, and much more. The food was wonderful, and everyone ate at the table. After we had finished eating, Grandma put me on her bed. Grandma's hair was in a bun. She looked good. She never talked to me, but she covered me with a sheer curtain to keep the flies off me. I felt so loved that day, thanks to my grandma and grandpa. This memory still brings a smile to my heart.

Now looking back, I believe Grandma was afraid of Mom and Bill. She was definitely afraid of Mom. Mom didn't seem upset about Grandpa being dead; she seemed glad she could do what she wanted.

I later found out that Grandpa was the one that kept Mom in her place and stopped her from walking over everyone else. Grandma was afraid of her daughter with good reason. Grandpa had sent Mom away many times when she was behaving badly.

We used Grandma's outside toilet before we left. We never had an inside toilet even we were living in the one-room apartment over the bar. Our toilet was down the hall and shared with all the other renters. We all got back in the car and drove around while Mom looked for a place for us to live. I guess Mom took Grandma's money when she went in the house. I wondered what Grandma would do without any money. I bet Mom took all she could find.

The next couple of years are mixed together, so my memories may be out of order. We found a house at Five Points, Ohio. We had no furniture, not even a bed, but it was still better than living by the river. We got one piece of furniture at a time. Some we found, and people gave us other pieces.

Mom had another baby and named him Jimmy. Mom was still with Bill off and on, and I can still hear him saying, "I'm going to Columbus to get a job. I'll come back and we'll all move there." Mom told me later that he would be gone for two or three months at a time.

Mom always went to town, to either Pomeroy or Middleport, once a week. She would leave us at home and hitchhike there. She would come back with some food, always drunk, and sometimes with a man. The food always tasted so good. I think we could have had some happy times except we never knew what to expect from Mom. She never stayed happy without a man in her life.

We enjoyed it best when Mom was with someone because she would forget about us. Sometimes when she went to town, she would be gone all night and come home the next day. She would sleep all day when she got home. She always brought food. This was very important to us. The food had to last all week.

Sometimes during the week, Mom would send me to a neighbor to borrow flour, eggs, or other things. Mom would mix the flour with water, fry it, and we would have fried bread to eat. In the summertime, we would pick greens and cook and eat them. Once we got a goat and named her Nanny. We could milk Nanny. Mom showed me how to milk, and it became my job. Mom would use the milk, flour, and sugar and make pudding. This was the best stuff in the whole world. We had Nanny for several months, and then she was gone. That was sad for Freddie and me because she was also our pet, a friend we loved and played with daily. We never knew what happened to Nanny. She was just gone one day.

Bill came back. This was always a hard time for me. He still took every opportunity to sexually abuse me. Bill was driving an old truck. He moved us back to an old house in Letart Falls about fifteen miles from Five Points.

Grandma Rosa came to live with us. Woodrow, Mom's youngest brother, drowned in the Ohio River while fishing, so Grandma was now alone with no place to call home. Grandma got an old-age pension check every month in the mail. Mom and Bill kept those checks and staying drunk and fighting all the time. Mom always had black eyes and a busted mouth.

One day the police came. Mom said someone had turned them in for something. She always felt someone was out to get her and usually blamed Pap for everything. She said Pap turned her in because he wanted to get Grandma's pension. After the police came, Grandma went to live with Aunt Mary, and Mom and Bill went to jail. Freddie, Jimmy, and I were taken to the Children's Home in Pomeroy, Ohio.

This time, our stay at the children's home was a short one, about six months. Mom and Bill got out of jail, we got out of the home, and we all moved to Bowman's Run. We moved into an old house that had no windows, no water, no electricity, and it sat on top of a hill. A creek ran on two sides of the house, and there was a footbridge across one of the creeks. None of the houses we lived in had electric service. We always used a kerosene lamp.

None of the houses we lived in had water either. That was one of my hardest jobs as a child, carrying water. I'm not sure how old I was when it became my job. I know I was carrying a bucket of water long before I started school. The bucket was big, and I would walk to the creek or a neighbor's house to fill it. I always started out with a full bucket of water, but by the time I got home, it was only about half full and I was soaking wet. My shoes would be soaked, and my arms would be hurting. In the winter, this was a more difficult task for me. I would be so cold and wet. I slipped on the snow and ice. If I arrived home without enough water, I was sent straight back for a refill no matter how cold, wet, or tired I was.

Living on Bowman's Run was hard for me. Not only did I have a long way to carry water, Mom also had a second assignment for me. She and Bill had discovered that a neighbor had a root cellar with canned jars of food.

After I had carried enough water, they sent me to steal a jar of food from the root cellar. Sometimes Mom and Bill sent me back several times. The canned food was mostly vegetables, but once in a while I would get a jar of fruit. It was so dark in the root cellar I couldn't see what I was getting. I was so little I could only carry two jars at a time, so I had to make numerous trips. I had to do my stealing while the family was away from home.

One time, Mom and Bill had been gone to town for at least two days and nights. Freddie, Jimmy, and I were so hungry. I went to the root cellar and got a jar of food. We had a hard time getting the jar opened. It took a long time, but I finally got it opened, and it was a jar of cherries. The jar had little white worms floating on top. I guess the person who canned the cherries didn't see the worms in the cherries. We didn't care; we were so hungry. I scooped the worms out and divided the cherries and we ate all of them. The cherries were so sour. I think they had been canned without any sugar. That was okay; when you're really hungry like we were, you will eat almost anything.

One thing I can say about my mother and the men in her life, especially Bill, is that they did not do any physical labor. They would sit by the fire and wait for us children to gather wood to keep them warm. Mom did not dirty her hands on such tasks.

Gathering wood was a cold job. Freddie and I would work all day hunting sticks to keep a fire going in the house for Mom and Bill. Sometimes it would be so cold I would give Freddie the wood I had found so he could go in the house for a few minutes and get warm. Sometimes our fingers would get so stiff it would be hard to move them, and we always had plenty of splinters in our hands. The little sticks we found burned quickly, so it was an all-day job for us.

Sometimes Bill would take the car, and we would all go to pick up sticks along the road. That was always better for Freddie and me. Sometimes we would go in the car and pick up coal that the big trucks lost beside the road. Coal burned longer than our sticks, so we usually saved it to burn at night.

Chapter 4
THE DIFFICULTIES OF LEARNING

One day, a man came to the house and told Mom I had to go to school. I found out later he was a truant officer. School had finally caught up with me. The next day, I got up, walked down the little hill across the footbridge, and waited there for the school bus. I did not wash my face, I did not comb my hair, I did not have anything to eat or drink, and I did not change my clothes. I'm not sure if I had any other clothes to change into. Seems like I always wore the clothes I slept in at night.

After I arrived at the school, I wandered the hallways for a while until someone told me which room was my classroom. The teacher was calling the roll. All the other children were in their seats. I just stood inside the door with my head down.

Then, to the best of my knowledge and memory, the teacher looked up at me. She was wearing glasses. She asked, "What's your name?" I told her my name, Erma. She said, "Erma, what's your last name?" I told her I didn't know my last name, and the other children laughed. The teacher then asked, "Where do you live?" I told her I didn't know, and the children laughed. I just hung my head. She said, "How old are you?" I did not reply, and the children laughed. She looked at me for what seemed like a long time and then told me to sit down.

My first day in the first grade was a scary, humiliating, and shameful day. This was a very hard time for me. I did not know anything and I couldn't learn anything. I think back to the other parents bringing their children to school, making sure they went to the correct classroom, talking to their teachers, carrying and paying for their children's lunches. I knew no one would ever be there for me for anything.

The bus seemed to make many stops, and I saw some parents waiting at the bus stops for their children. I was afraid I would miss my stop, and I knew no one would be waiting for me. The bus stopped again. The driver said, "This is it." I looked up; I could see his eyes looking at me in the mirror. I got off the bus and walked to the footbridge.

I remember thinking, *what are we going to do?* I always talked to my guardian angel in my mind. I sat down at the footbridge to think. No one would wonder why I wasn't home yet; no one would give it a thought. I kept thinking about the white house with the green wood around the windows. I had a hard time talking to people or asking anyone for help. Mostly I did my best to avoid any type of communication with anyone, including my family.

I knew I needed some adult help to get through this school thing. Mom had made it clear I had to go to school every day so she wouldn't go to jail.

At school, I had gone to the bathroom and there was a big mirror in there. I thought about how big it was—and that was me. My hair was messy and in my eyes. My dress was dirty, and one side was longer than the other was because I had pulled the hem out. There were holes on each side of my dress because I had pulled the long strings out. They kept getting in my way, and I couldn't tie them. My shoes were dirty, and I had no shoestrings. There was a hole over the big toe of one shoe. I looked so bad; no wonder the children at school laughed and made fun of me. In my own mind, I was so ugly.

There were several houses in sight but I was sure in my heart that I needed to go to the white house with the green wood around the windows. My guardian angel was telling me to go to that house, so instead of going home, I got up and started walking toward the white house. I went down the road and then up onto the porch. I could see through the screen because the door was open. A woman was singing and playing the piano. I recognized the song. It was "When the Roll Is Called Up Yonder." I didn't knock. I just sat on the porch and listened. I thought it was like being in church when I was in the children's home in Columbus. I felt safe. The singing stopped, and I wanted to run home, but she was at the door watching me.

I stood up. I said, "My name is Erma. I need to go to school every day and I have no clothes. Do you have any clothes for me and can I go to church with you?" She seemed to look at me forever. She asked me if I was the little girl that lived up on the hill. I nodded my head yes. She told me to come in and that she had been thinking about me.

Her daughter was older than I was and had lots of clothes too little for her to wear. The woman gave me some food to eat and a bag of food to take home. She put the bag of clothes, the bag of food, and me in her car and took me home. As I was getting out of the car, she said that on Sunday morning at 9:15 I could go to church with her.

I felt like a princess with all the nice clothes and shoes. I went down to the creek every morning and washed my face and hands. The schoolchildren still made fun of me but not as much because now I blended in more. I went to Sunday school every week with Brenda and her daughter, Mary. In the car together, Mary and I would laugh and talk, but during school, Mary acted like she didn't know me. That was okay because she was in a higher grade and I only saw her in the morning at recess.

Lunchtime was almost unbearable for me because the free lunch program had not begun. They cooked the school lunch in the kitchen, and the aromas were wonderful. My stomach would make noise. I never had breakfast and sometimes didn't have dinner, so I was always hungry.

At lunchtime, I always asked to go to the bathroom. Some children would line up for lunch in the lunchroom, and the children who brought their lunch would eat at their desks. After eating, they went outside for recess. I would go to the bathroom and then go outside to play. Mom never sent a lunch for me.

Mom had another baby and named her Jeannie. Now there were four of us. The next few days were very hard for me. I could not go to school for three days. I had to stay home to take care of Freddie and Jimmy because they were not old enough to go to school. I had to stay with them while Mom was in the hospital.

Bill was also home at this time, and I was his entertainment. I did not want to hate him, but he was so dirty and nasty. Finally Mom came home from the hospital with a baby girl, and I went back to school.

I became very close to Freddie and Jimmy at this time. We didn't play with Jeannie. My heart breaks when I think of her. Jeannie was treated like an animal. I look back now and ask why I didn't do more. It seemed like all I could do was keep my head above water.

I do want to elaborate more about Jeannie. Mom never held her. I cannot remember Mom feeding Jeannie or putting a diaper on her. Mom would not let us talk to or play with Jeannie. Mom said she was afraid we would hurt the baby. I finally began to realize that Mom didn't like Jeannie. Jeannie started sitting up, and she was on the floor all the time now. She ate on the floor and slept sitting up with her head between her legs.

It was a repeat of my first memories at Aunt Mary's. The voice and the words, and the *you are not important, you don't count, you are nobody* attitude. This is how Jeannie was treated on a daily basis.

First grade was bad, but second grade was better because of a wonderful teacher, Mrs. Buck. She seemed to understand what I was going through.

Mrs. Buck always ate her lunch at her desk. One morning, she called me to her desk and said she had a lunch for me. She pointed to the windowsill and there sat a sack lunch with my name on it. She said there would be a sack lunch there for me every day. I never wanted to miss a day of school because of the wonderful things that were in my lunch each day.

One day, my teacher wasn't at school and I had no lunch that day. The next day, Mrs. Buck told me if she was ever absent again, I was to tell the substitute that I had a sack lunch in the bottom drawer. She opened the bottom drawer and showed me the sack with my name on it. The sack was filled with wonderful things that would last for a long time. The children made fun of me, but I didn't care. I loved my teacher, I wanted to be near her all the time, and I wanted to make her proud of me.

On Valentine's Day, she handed me a bag of valentines with all the children's names already on the cards. All I had to do was write my name twenty-nine times. I wrote my name on each one. There was even a card that said To My Teacher. I signed my name just for her. I was so thrilled.

One day, when the weather was getting colder, my teacher showed me where all the other children hung their coats. Under my name, the most beautiful coat in the whole wide world was hanging. She said it was mine, to keep me warm.

Mrs. Buck made me feel special and loved. She seemed to know what was happening to me and cared about me as a person. She was the greatest. Thank you, Mrs. Buck, for being my teacher.

We moved to Racine, between Pomeroy and Letart Falls. We lived in a building with a little short room added on. Big people couldn't stand up in the short room. The building we lived in had been a chicken coop.

Nelson ran the farm, and he drank all the time with Mom and Bill. Nelson said Mom and Bill could live there and work the farm. They had met him in a bar in Middleport. Nelson's wife was nice but she never came out of the house. She had something wrong with her.

Bill didn't stay long. He left for Columbus to get a job. He said he would be back. My mom was sleeping with Nelson, and they would fight in the milk barn just like Bill and Mom. Sometimes Nelson and Mom would go for days without speaking to each other. They had bottles hidden everywhere and drank on a daily basis. Mom still made her weekly visits to town if she and Nelson weren't speaking to each other.

Freddie started school. I was in the third grade, and Jeannie was about two years old. She spent all her time on the floor and couldn't walk or talk. She did not cry much. And Mom was going to have another baby.

Nelson wanted us to move, so Bill came back and we moved to Bowman's Run again. That was a really bad move. The house was falling in. It was winter, and when the wind blew, the rug would raise up off the floor from the wind coming up between the cracks. We had a big round stove, but it was still so cold. The only way to get warm was to stay next to the stove and sleep in your coat, so that's what we did.

Freddie, Jimmy, and I were still in charge of going outside in the cold to gather sticks and pieces of wood to keep the fire burning. On this particular day, it was freezing and Freddie and Jimmy were so cold they had a hard time moving. I gave them the wood I had gathered and told them to go in the house. Mom and Bill wouldn't yell at them because they would be bringing in wood for the fire. I turned to pick up a piece of wood and stepped on a broken bottle. A sharp edge went into my anklebone. Blood was everywhere. I remember thinking, *I'm going to die.* I wondered if it was warm in heaven. I wondered what I was going to do because it was so cold outside, and it wouldn't be long before I got too cold to move. Then my companion in my heart said, "You can walk. Take your other sock off and tie it around your ankle and let's go!" I did as I was told. I was so glad to get inside the door.

I knew my foot was in bad shape, and everyday it got worse. I couldn't put my weight on it, and it ran fluid all the time and kept my sock wet. Each day was painful, and one day my leg was hot and red and the pain was unbearable. I asked the teacher if I could go to go to the bathroom. In the bathroom, I just fell to the floor and started crying. I couldn't stop. At some point, my teacher sent someone to the bathroom to check on me. The girl took one look at me and ran out. My teacher came in and told me to stay where I was. She left and got someone else. They put me in a car and took me home. They told me to stay in the car while they went in to see Mom. When they came out, they took me to the hospital. My foot still hurt, but it was warm in the hospital and the food was wonderful. The bed was so clean and soft. I don't know how long I stayed in the hospital, but when I came home I had a little crutch.

Another problem we had as little children was getting sick. Neglected and abused children deal with this problem differently than normal families. First of all, Mom never recognized any illness in her children. Should a problem arise with us, Mom merely saw it as an inconvenience to her or an aggravation. Mom only recognized Mom's needs. She never gave us so much as an aspirin. We didn't have a bed, and Mom had no love to spare. She still had us do our chores no matter how sick we were.

The only time Mom got serious about one of us being sick would be when someone at school or a neighbor saw one of us looking ill and would call social services and Barbara would appear. Mom hated Barbara and blamed her for her every trip to jail. Mom probably hated me more than she hated Barbara.

Bill and Mom picked me up at the hospital, and Mom was furious with me. She said we had to move again because of me. She said now they would be after her and she would go to jail again because of me.

Mom and Bill went into a bar after picking me up at the hospital. They left Freddie, Jimmy, Jeannie, and me sitting in the car. When they came out of the bar, they were with Nelson. The next day, we moved back to Nelson's farm.

Mom had another baby. She named him Bobby. Now there were five children—Freddie, Jimmy, Jeannie, Bobby, and me. We had moved back into the chicken coop with the little room on the back. I went to school and had the same teacher I had before.

Mom and Bill were drinking and fighting every day. We children knew that the best thing for us was to stay out of their way, out of sight. All of us except Jeannie could stay out of reach.

Bill and Mom were mean drunks. Bill would pick on Jeannie, and Mom would watch. I remember him jerking her up and trying to make her stand. He called her lazy. He tried to make her walk by hitting her on her legs, back, and bottom. She fell many times, and he would jerk her up again and repeat the beating. She had blood coming out of her mouth. I didn't remember hearing Jeannie crying. I don't think she ever cried.

I couldn't stand seeing her being tortured. She was just a little girl. She was so helpless. I ran outside crying and stayed out there for a long time. I could still hear Bill yelling at Jeannie. I wanted my guardian angel to leave my heart and go be with Jeannie. That did not happen.

Chapter 5
My Tattoo and My Barbara

We didn't live on Nelson's farm for very long this time, but I sure have a lot of memories. Mom and Bill were staying drunk. One night they came home with some needles, ink, and a full box of matches. Bill said he knew how to make tattoos. Mom was his first victim, if you could ever call her a victim. She was drunk and kept saying it didn't hurt. Bill made a heart on Mom's arm and put his name in the heart. I watched this strange process, amazed at what I was seeing. This was the last time I needed a lesson about hanging around when they were doing something.

I remember the exact second the thought came into Bill's head. He looked up at me and said he was going to put a tattoo on my arm. I backed up and shook my head no. He told me to sit down and quit being a big chicken. Bill started on my arm, but it bled so much that he had to stop. He had to adjust the needles so they wouldn't go in my arm too deep. My arm was smaller than Mom's arm.

The tattoo process was simple jailhouse art. You put needles around a matchstick with the needles sticking out farther than the match. Tie these all together so they don't move. Stick the ends of the needles in to ink. Bill used India ink. You stick the needles in your arm or where ever you are putting your tattoo. You just continue dipping and piercing until you have completed your word or the design of your choice.

Back to my tattoo. I remember tasting my salty tears. I did not make a sound; I knew better. It would not take much to make Bill angry at me, and my punishment would have been horrible. It always was when he got mad; everyone suffered. Bill was going to put U.S.A. on my arm, but he only got U.S. on before Mom flew into a rage. He and Mom began fighting and became very physical with each other.

I slipped out quietly and quickly. I went to the barn, and luckily no one was there. Nelson liked little girls too. I knew if I hid myself under the hay, I would be warm and safe. I wasn't alone; my guardian angel was with me. I stayed in the barn all night, and that was not my first time. I felt safely hidden, the hay was warm, and my arm was really hurting.

Bill had an old car and was working in a junkyard in Pomeroy. He would come home with a lot of parts in the trunk. I think they were alternators. He would build a big fire in the stove and throw the parts in the fire. Then he would take them out when they were red-hot and pound them with a hammer to get the copper. Every Friday, Bill and Mom would go sell the copper wire.

I was having a hard time in school. Everything was a blur. I could not read or write, and sometimes I couldn't even spell my name. My mind wasn't working right, but I think I was in the third grade.

We had lived at Bowman's Run two times, Five Points one time, and this was our third time at Nelsons—all in about three years.

I had taken my books home from school and never returned them. We had moved over a weekend, and I didn't know what happened to the books. The day I returned to school, my teacher asked me where my books were. I told her I didn't know, so she became angry with me and told me I could not have any more books. She told me I had to stand by my desk every recess and every lunch period until I returned my books to her. I really did not know where my books were or what happened to them. Mom or Bill could have used them to start a fire. They were always looking for paper to start a fire.

My teacher was so upset about her books and treated me like I no longer existed. This was okay with me, but I did get tired of standing by my desk.

On Thursday, May 3, 1956, I went to school. I was still standing by my desk during recess and lunch break because of my missing books. The bell rang for us to have recess, and my teacher told me we were going to the principal's office. I thought it was about the books I had lost, and I was very afraid I would get a whipping for the missing books.

In the office was a tall, sandy-haired woman with the kindest eyes I have ever seen. Her eyes were the color of the sky. I had seen her before. She had talked with me at the children's home several times. One time, she came to our house and brought me clothes and shoes.

On this day, she said to me, "Hi, Erma, my name is Barbara. Do you remember me?" I nodded my head yes. She handed me a bag and told me she had brought my lunch. I remember I thanked her. I couldn't wait to see what was inside. As usual, I'd had no breakfast that morning. Barbara then asked how I felt. I said okay. Then she looked at my teacher and asked if she could talk to me alone. The principal and the teacher left the office.

Barbara asked me if I liked school. I told her no. I told her I had to stand at my desk every day because I lost my books the last time we moved. She said she would pay for my books and I wouldn't have to stand by my desk anymore.

Barbara told me she was worried about me. She asked if I needed anything. I told her no. She asked me what happened to my arm. I looked at my arm. It hurt. It was red and swollen, and yellow fluid was running out of my tattoo. I told her that Bill had put it on my arm. Barbara told me we were going to go to see a doctor about my tattoo.

The doctor cleaned and wrapped my arm. He gave me a shot and a tube of cream to put on it to make it feel better. Then Barbara took me back to school. It was lunchtime. She took me to my classroom, told me good-bye, and kissed my cheek. I started standing by my desk, but Barbara told me to sit down and eat my lunch. She went to my teacher and talked to her. Barbara was only there for a short time, but in that short amount of time she made my world a much better place.

My arm felt so much better, and I knew to take the bandage off my arm before I went home. Mom and Bill could never know that Barbara had visited me at school, and they couldn't know she had taken me to the doctor for my tattooed arm. Mom hated Barbara. We would probably move quickly if Mom found out about Barbara's visit.

At the last recess, I went outside, took the bandage off, and put dirt all over my tattoo so it looked like it did that morning when I left for school. I was afraid of what was going to happen. Something always happened when Barbara came around. She had taken a picture of my arm.

Freddie and I always sat next to each other on the school bus. Today he told me a woman came to see him and brought him a lunch. I knew who it was, and together we decided not to tell Mom.

I later found out that Barbara had left the school that day and went straight to the Pomeroy courthouse to file a petition to have all of us children permanently removed from Mom and Bill. This petition was to be served the following Monday, but so much happened over the weekend that this didn't happen. Everything came to a head that weekend.

I did not know my life with Mom was coming to an end. If I had known, I wonder if I would have done anything different. Freddie and I did not go to school the next morning. Mom had us stay home so she and Bill could leave earlier to sell the copper wire. Bobby was about eight weeks old. Jeannie was about three years old. I think Jimmy was about five, and Freddie was about six and a half years old. I was about nine years old.

This is how I remember the events that led to Mom and Bill going to prison, and us children going to the children's home.

Chapter 6
ALONE, HUNGRY, AND SCARED

Friday, Mom and Bill left. Bobby was crying all the time. I don't remember changing his diapers or even if we had any diapers for him. I do know we did not have any food and we were all hungry. We were five small children, alone, cold, and hungry. We went inside and I could not get the kerosene lamp lit so we all huddled together in the dark.

Saturday, everyone was very hungry. I told Freddie and Jimmy to go to the corncrib and get some corn and crack it with a hammer and eat it. They did. I went down to the barn and got some cow feed. We all ate this feed. Jeannie seemed to like it. It tasted kind of nutty.

Bobby was still crying, and he was very hot to touch. I decided to milk Nelson's cow and give Bobby the milk. I knew how to milk because I had milked Nanny. I knew how to get the cow in the barn, get her feed, and get her in the milking stall. I was able to do this, and I got enough milk for all of us to have some.

Saturday night, I still couldn't get the lamp lit, so we again huddled together in the dark. Something was really wrong with Bobby. He was sleeping more and crying less. He was really hot.

Sunday morning, I decided to kill a chicken. We were starving. I got Mom's big pot and built a fire in the stove. Freddie and Jimmy had a hard time catching the chicken. It took a long time. I killed the chicken and tried to pull out the feathers. I couldn't get very many out. I waited for the water to get hot, and then I put the red chicken in the pot, feathers, feet, guts, and all. We let it cook for a long time.

We all ate the chicken except for Bobby. There was a lot of meat on the chicken, and we all felt better after we ate. I think we were okay except for Bobby. Bobby was really sick. By late Sunday afternoon, he was sleeping all the time. I thought he was dying. Mom had been gone since around noon on Friday.

Where was Mom? I knew that even if she came home now she would be in no shape to help Bobby. I knew she would come through that door fighting with Bill or some other man and would eventually pass out for the rest of the day. Whenever and however she came home, she would not help Bobby. I had to do something now.

We had a neighbor who lived up the road. I had not met her or ever spoken to her, but I knew I had to go to her for help because Bobby was dying. I ran up the road and knocked on her door. A woman came and opened the door. I said, "Please come and help me. My baby brother is dying. My mom is gone. Please come help me." She told me to get in her car, and she drove down to our house. She went in and looked at Bobby. She told me not to touch him and said she would be right back. She came back and brought washcloths and water and began washing Bobby's face and arms.

I heard sirens in the distance. They were getting closer. The ambulance came to our house, and a police car followed. Medics began rushing around, working with Bobby. I don't think they even saw Jeannie on the floor until later. One of the officers told Freddie, Jimmy, and me to sit on the grass outside out of the way until they could talk with us.

About this time, Bill drove up in his car. Mom wasn't with him. The police officers started talking to Bill. Soon, another police car drove up, and Mom was in this car and so was Barbara. Mom was very drunk and she had bags of food.

I found out later that she and Bill had gotten into a fight. Bill had left her and come on home. Mom was walking home with the food as the police car with Barbara was driving by on its way to our house. Barbara said she saw a woman very drunk, staggering down the road. She asked the police officer to slow down, and she recognized Mom and had the officer pick her up and bring her to the house.

As soon as Mom got out of the police car, she attacked Bill. She beat on him until the police got her off him and wrestled her down to the ground and handcuffed her hands behind her back. She thought Bill had called the police.

The ambulance left with Bobby, its sirens blaring. Someone said Jeannie needed to go to the hospital. Everyone was talking and rushing around. Barbara's car left with Jeannie for the hospital.

The officers and others were still talking to Bill. They took Mom away in a police car with her hands cuffed behind her back. Mom was still behaving badly.

Soon everyone was gone. They left Bill, Freddie, Jimmy, and me sitting in the yard. I had been through this many times. I knew Barbara would return for us when the emergencies were handled. What a mess! I wished I could just disappear. I had followed my heart to save Bobby. The lady I went to for help had brought all these people.

The next morning, Bill made sure we went to school. As soon as I got to school, I asked the teacher if I could go to the post office. It was beside the school, and she often let children take items to the postmaster. I was still surprised when she said I could go.

I went out the door and started down the road. I walked from Racine to Aunt Mary's and Pap's. I remember it was late afternoon when I arrived. Aunt Mary and Grandma Rosa met me on the porch. Aunt Mary asked what I doing there, and Grandma told me to go back to Mom because there wasn't enough food to feed everyone.

I told Aunt Mary that the police had taken Mom to jail. Aunt Mary said they would let Mom out and she would come for me. Grandma and Aunt Mary went into the house while I sat in the tire swing under a big tree and ate some grapes I had picked from the vines on the fence row. A car drove up to the gate and Barbara got out. She told me she and a policeman had driven to our house where he arrested Bill, and she had taken Jimmy to the Meigs County Children's Home. When she had arrived to school to check on me, she learned I had run away, and assumed I had gone to Aunt Mary's. Barbara told me Freddie was very upset at school. She had to call a police officer to take him to the Children's Home. She pleaded with me to help with my little brothers, but I told her I wanted to stay at Pap's. I knew my brothers and was sure Barbara was telling the truth. Most people could not understand what Freddie was saying because he could not speak well. He had always had a serious speech problem. He didn't trust people, and he was angry. He wouldn't sit at his desk in school, so they just left him alone. Freddie wasn't mean or bad. If you just left him alone, he was quiet. The only reason Freddie went to school was because of Bill. Freddie knew Bill would beat him if he caused any problems.

At the Children's Home, Barbara said Freddie was in a corner with a big stick and wouldn't let anyone near him or Jimmy. I knew they were afraid. Barbara said if I would come and help her with them she would let me come back to Pap's later. So I went with Barbara.

I remember when I first saw Freddie and Jimmy they were so scared and seemed so alone. I felt so much love for them. They both ran to me, and I sat down. They sat so close to me they were almost sitting in my lap.

In our short lives, Mom had never showed us any kindness or love. We never had a soft hug, a kiss, or any type of warm affection from Mom. We had wanted her love more than anything, and it never happened.

The next day was one of the worst in my life. They took all kinds of pictures of us and asked all kinds of questions. We were all taken to the doctor.

I was questioned at great length about Bill's behavior toward me. Had he bothered me sexually? Had he touched me? Where did he touch me? I think they already knew the answers to their questions. My replies were always the same. I never told them anything. I always ended up with Mom and Bill, and I didn't want to be punished for anything I told the authorities.

Meigs County Children's Home (original 1882) *The following is copied from historical documents and newspapers printed in the 1880's.*

At the spring election of 1882, the citizens of the count voted to erect a Children's Home (with barn and other outbuildings) at the cost of $10,000. A site was selected on 25 acres of ground, buildings erected, and was ready for occupancy in the spring of 1883.

The farm is in good condition, and is favorably located in a good neighborhood, is sufficiently retired, yet easy of access, and from the buildings and grounds is presented a beautiful and picturesque view.

The object is to afford an asylum to indigent children of the county under the age of sixteen years, until suitable homes can be provided for them, with kindly disposed persons, and all reasonable efforts are made for their improvement in industrious habits and morals while they remain in the Home. As one newspaper stated, 'The ulterior object of the Children Home is to bring up children to be good and useful citizens, who would otherwise be paupers and criminals.' The building was planned with large airy rooms for a home-like atmosphere. (History of Meigs County Book)

Chapter 7
Mom's Arrest—My Fault

Once the state took over Mom's five children, it was out with the old and in with the new, and more of the same. Pictures were taken of all of us. I think I was in fair shape except for my tattooed arm. It was still infected. Freddie was in fair shape; he had bruises and a speech problem. People began calling him Dego. Jimmy was in fair shape. He would not talk and was very scared. He was underweight.

I believe Jeannie was about three years old. She was in bad shape. She was starving, had no hair, couldn't talk, walk, or stand. She had rickets. She had spent her short life on the floor, and she slept with her head between her legs. Her back had formed wrong. The safety pins holding her diaper had rusted to her skin. Jeannie was in the hospital for a long time.

Bobby was the saddest of all of us. He was about two months old, starving, and he had double pneumonia. Bobby had feces, wet and dried, all up his back and was covered in sores. He was dying.

Bobby never came to the Pomeroy Children's Home. He was sent to a special hospital in Columbus because of his condition, and then he was taken to a children's home in Columbus when he was released from the hospital. This home took care of little babies. The home in Pomeroy only took children that could take care of themselves. I never saw Bobby until years later.

Now there were four of Mom's children, not five. We children did not go in the courtroom. We sat on a bench in a long hallway. Freddie, Jimmy, and

I were alone. A door opened, and a policeman came in the hallway. Mom was with him.

Mom saw me and made a run for me. I could see how mad she was and that she was out of control. I knew that look; I had seen it many times. Mom was trying to get to me to hit me, but the policeman caught her before she could. She was screaming and cursing at me. The policeman kept telling Mom to stay away from us, but she kept trying to break away from him to get to me.

Mom was saying everything was my fault. She said she hated me and wished I was dead. She was out of control. Another policeman came, and they put her on the floor and handcuffed her hands behind her back. They picked her up and took her away. The officers could stop Mom from hitting me, but they couldn't keep her from saying how she felt about me.

Mom was gone, and it was no secret that she hated me and wanted me dead. What had I done? Barbara came and put her arm around me. She kept saying everything would be okay.

Deep down inside me, I knew things would never be okay. I needed to cry, but I would do that later when I was alone. I wanted—I needed to be alone. My mommy was gone and she hated me.

Mom had ripped, torn, and shredded my heart, my soul, my very being. All that remained was a shell of a little girl, just a shell. I will forever be that little girl.

Meigs County Children's Home was not equipped to handle children with handicaps. There were no accommodations for children who couldn't walk. Jeannie was released from the hospital, and she had to come to the home to live with us. Certain things had to be changed because Jeannie could not walk. Barbara explained to me that they would take my bed and put it against the wall so Jeannie could sleep with me and not fall out of bed. They put two beds together to make a bed for us. This way, Jeannie would be safe. Barbara also said I would not be going back to school since there were only six weeks or so of school left for that year. I would be staying at the home taking care of Jeannie.

The home was a wonderful place at first. We had three meals a day, we had clothes, clean clothes, we had our own clean bed with covers, and we had a bath every night. I know this is unbelievable and hard to understand, but I missed my mommy. I was old enough to know that the judge had said we would never see Mom again. I felt like she had died. I cried every night for a long time thinking about her. What did they do to her? It was entirely my fault.

I remember the first time people came to the home to take a child home with them. This is the most frightening event I can remember at the home. We were told to dress in our Sunday clothes. We lined up for the visitors to check us out. They would walk past us, stop in front of a child, and ask their name or how old they were. That night, I went downstairs to the dining room for dinner. I didn't see Jimmy. He was gone like Bobby. Someone had taken my little brother.

Now there were only three.

I remember thinking, *why did they take Jimmy? Why would they take my little brother? Will he be safe? What did they want from him?*

People took children for all kinds of reasons. Some of the reasons we may never know or understand. Big boys and girls were often taken to work in the fields. Some people took small children to fulfill a parenting instinct. It seemed mostly that the women wanted to be parents and the husbands had other reasons.

Money was also a good reason to take in a poor homeless child. The state paid the foster families for each child they took home. The qualifications for being a foster parent were not as strict then as they are today.

I heard the other girls talking at night about some of the foster homes. They told horrible stories. Some of the girls had been severely sexually abused. They talked about the hard work they were forced to do on the farms. Many of the girls had been in homes where you were only given a certain amount to eat. Several of the homes gave severe beatings where the bruises wouldn't show. A foster child's life was not easy.

At this point in my life, I trusted no one. Everyone wanted something from me. I had nothing to give to anyone. I was only a shell of a little girl.

The next Saturday, a man and woman came to the home for the children's lineup. They wanted a baby. Jeannie was the youngest, so after lunch, I had to help pack Jeannie's things. The man and woman drove away with my little sister.

Now there were two, Freddie and I.

I went under the porch and cried. I had such strong feelings of desperation. I'm not sure anyone can understand the shock, the terror, the full weight of the responsibility I felt for what was happening to my family. The fear I felt for each of my brothers and sister gave me more stress than most adults deal with in a lifetime. The greatest blow of all was to know it was my fault because my mother had said so.

I was afraid someone would pick me, and I was also terrified I would be alone forever. I felt like I was disappearing. I felt powerless. Before, my mother would eventually come back and get me. This time I knew there was no chance of her ever coming back. I would never see her again. I wondered if they took her away and killed her. Why else would they say we would never see her again? I could have asked, but I wasn't sure I wanted to know.

At the home, they told me when to eat, when to go to bed, what rooms I could go into, and when I could go outside. I wondered what would happen if someone did not follow the rules. I soon got an answer. Two boys got into a fight, and Mr. G. took off his belt and whipped both of them. I didn't want anything to do with Mr. G. and his belt. I was afraid of him.

Everyone at the home had a job. My job was to bathe the small children and get them ready for bed. I started helping the first- and second-grade boys and girls get ready for their baths and bed immediately after dinner.

After their baths, they brushed their teeth and went to the TV room. There were two TV rooms, one for boys and one for the girls. They watched TV until 7 PM and then went to bed. The older children went to bed at 8 PM on weeknights and 9 PM on weekends.

During that time, I felt very strange and empty inside. It was as if I was disappearing. I had no friends, and I trusted no one.

From the girls' dorm room, there was a door that opened to the side porch. I discovered a secret place under the porch. It was like I was hiding from the world. It was the only place I had found where I could have alone time.

I looked around at the children living in the home. Most of them had been there for a long time. They were the castoffs of society that no one wanted. These children had things wrong with them, things that you could see when you looked at them: physical deformities, obesity, or maybe they were just unpleasant to look at. These were the children in the home with me. Some of the children had obvious mental problems and would never be among the chosen. Even at my age, that was so sad and depressing.

I continued to go under the porch. I would stay there from breakfast until lunchtime. I tried to work things out in my head. Even now, I find myself spending hours just sitting and trying to find solutions.

One thing I decided under the porch was that I would sit with my back to the boys' table so I would not know when my brother, my last brother, had been picked and taken away.

Meigs County Courthouse – *This is the hallway on the first floor where me and two of my younger brothers sat waiting for Mom's court day. They brought Mom through this door and past us as she came from the jail to the courtroom.*

Meigs County Jail – *Located right beside the courthouse. The cement platform on the left is where they walked Mom over through the side door.*

Chapter 8
MY FAMILY OF STICKS

I went under the porch more and more. I began picking up sticks and pretending. Soon the sticks became people—a mother named Mary Jane and a father named Clell. There were three brothers: Wesley, Jimmy, and Bobby. The family decided they wanted a little girl, and the boys wanted a little sister.

This family went to the children's home and chose from the lineup. As they walked past the children, Wesley pointed and said he wanted the little girl with the orange hair. That little girl was me. That's the day a little girl joined the family. Her name was Erma. She was very small with orange hair and green eyes. All the family loved her very much.

The stick family lived in a little white house. They had two cars because Wesley could drive. All of my stick family loved each other, and Wesley didn't let anyone hurt his little sister. Mary Jane would buy pretty dresses for Erma. She also made special lunches for Erma to take to school.

School had started again, but this time I was different. I would put on my new dress that Mary Jane bought for me. I felt as good and as pretty as any of the other girls. I opened my lunch at school. It was not the peanut butter sandwich that the people at the home prepared. It was a lunch Mary Jane had prepared for her little Erma. It could be lunchmeat, cheese, cookies, and potato chips—whatever Erma liked.

In the mornings, I would fix my hair like Mary Jane did under the porch.

I walked and talked like Mary Jane's Erma. People started to notice me. They told me I looked nice. I never looked uncared for again.

My life was built under that side porch. I was pretty and happy, and it showed. When people would tease me, make me sad, or hurt me, I would escape as fast as possible under the porch, and when I came out, I was Mary Jane and Clell's little girl and no one hurt me. My wonderful family protected me.

My stick family began as make-believe. I couldn't wait to get under the porch with my family that loved me so. I started to manipulate people to get more time under the porch for myself. I learned that the best way to get what I wanted was to put up a good front. Nobody did their job as well as I did.

I was never on kitchen duty because the little children loved having me put them to bed and tell them bedtime stories. I never went to the TV room. I stayed upstairs with the little boys to help keep them quiet. I wasn't a problem to anyone. I did extra things for the staff and children whenever I had the time. I learned to be a good liar. My goal was to get what I wanted and never let anyone use me or interfere with the life I was building for myself.

I never told anyone about my make-believe family. No one ever knew I was playing a part. In my mind, the unreal became the real. The real became the unreal. I was on stage. I loved my family and I loved being under the porch. This was my safe world, under the porch.

I began building my life with the sticks. I didn't miss Mom anymore. I didn't miss anyone. I was the new Erma who only wore the prettiest dresses, who had her hair fixed just so. I always had the best lunches prepared with love by Mary Jane, my pretend Mommy.

Chapter 9
NOBODY TELLS

One evening when we all went to dinner in the dining hall, Mr. G. told us all to turn our chairs away from the table. He said we could not eat or go anywhere until he found out who broke the window in Barbara's office. We had to sit in the dining room for a long time.

I remember thinking what would happen to the person who broke the window. I was wondering what we needed to do to take care of this problem. It was while I was sitting and thinking that I realized I didn't have my guardian angel with me because he didn't answer my question when I didn't know what to do. I was alone, all alone. Mr. G. said that if he didn't find out who broke the window, he would whip each one of us with the belt. I needed an answer to solve this immediate problem. None came. My guardian angel had left me. My special spirit that guided and took care of me was gone, but so was that Erma. Sitting there was not Erma, but make-believe Erma.

Finally, a boy stood up and told Mr. G. that another boy had thrown a rock at him and the rock had hit the window, breaking it. Only the boy who broke the window got a whipping and no dinner. The next day, the boy who told was beaten up and hurt. It was one of the unwritten laws of the home: *nobody tells on anybody*.

Mr. and Mrs. G. ran a strict orphanage. Everything ran on time, and everybody worked. There were between twenty and thirty children of all ages. Some of the children were mean, and no one messed with them. We had our own rules. We had an entire underworld that the staff knew nothing about.

I realized that anytime you have a group like this, you will have leaders and victims. I didn't have it in me to be mean or to hurt others and I was never going to be a victim again if I could help it. So I became the pretty one with long and shiny hair, a beautiful smile, sweet and kind to all. I was the one the boys all liked, but I was careful to keep my distance, I became an excellent liar, a manipulator of great schemes, and a sweet, innocent flirt.

The girls were allowed to have one Sunday outfit, two play outfits, two pairs of shoes, three school outfits, and underwear. We could not have anything extra. We were not allowed to have makeup. The clothes were kept on the third floor, or what some people would call the attic of the children's home. Clothing was the only thing allowed on this floor. It was like a used clothing store with all kinds and sizes of girls' and boys' clothes.

It became my job to take the new children up to the third floor to get them clothes. I got this job by being helpful. Mrs. G. could depend on me because I was so reliable and pleasant.

I used all my skills to achieve my goals for Erma. I took full advantage of my position to dress Erma as she should be dressed, only in the best available. While I had the new girl try on her clothes, I would check out the newly available for Erma. Finding something new and something that I liked was always a treat. I would put this aside in a special place for later. Somehow, I ended up with an extra key for the third floor. I also used this to my advantage.

On weekends, beginning Friday afternoon, we had a substitute staff. The weekends were busy, and the children gave the substitutes a hard time. The subs were kept busy downstairs. Only the strictest subs survived these weekends.

This was my time to take care of Erma's special needs. As always, I was kind and helpful to the subs. I bathed the little children on the second floor as usual. The only thing different was that I would wear the outfit I didn't want anymore.

While I was bathing the children, I would run upstairs to the third floor and use my extra key to gain entry. I would remove my old clothes and replace them with my cute new outfit. I was always careful to hang my old outfit in its proper place. Everything had to be in its proper place. That was a strict rule at the home. Should someone notice my new outfit, I would lie to them, something about a rip and Mrs. G. telling me to get something else.

Remember the rule—*no one ever tells on anyone else.* I never had more than my allowed outfits in my closet. Remember too, I always followed the rules. I was the helpful, sweet one.

The strict rules at the home helped me to feel safe. I would talk and flirt with the boys at school and on the bus, but at the home, we were not allowed to speak to the boys. We were not even allowed to speak to our brothers if we passed them in the hallway. Sometimes we did talk, but we were always very careful. Getting caught meant getting the belt or worse for both.

Girls were permitted to go outside only through the side door, and girls were allowed only in the side yard. The boys exited from the other side door and could only be in the opposite side yard from the girls. No one was permitted in the front or back of the building.

I remember one time a boy tried to hug me as I was coming downstairs from giving the little boys their bath. I don't believe anyone had touched me for weeks, maybe even months. His touching me made me feel sick inside. I could not stand for anyone to touch me in any form. I always pulled away from others.

There's a feeling that comes over me whenever anyone attempts to touch me. I want to put my hands up and stop them, keep them at a safe distance from me. Sometimes I still get a hug or am touched. I freeze. I can't respond. I want to scream, "Get away from me!" I still have these feelings and thoughts today. *Please keep your distance, don't touch me.* Whenever someone surprises me by touching me or taking my hand, I try to act normal, but if it's sudden, I jerk away. This has been a problem for me my entire life. I'm more comfortable being the one who reaches out.

Mr. and Mrs. G. trusted me. I had more freedom than any of the other children. They knew that whenever I had extra free time I wanted to be under the porch. She had asked me why I wanted to be there, and of course I lied to her. I told her I liked to read and couldn't think if there was any noise. She seemed okay with my answer and let me go as often as possible. I have often wondered what she would think if she knew I couldn't read.

I could not understand what the teachers wanted from me, and I could not learn. In first grade, my teacher spent a great deal of time trying to teach me to print with my right hand. It seemed that my mind could not deal with anything regarding spelling, writing, reading, or math. I believed I was going to remain ignorant all my life. In my heart, I believed I was dumb and would stay that way.

I remember thinking how silly the teachers were when they would tell me how important it was to do a page of arithmetic—when I hadn't eaten lunch or breakfast or had any dinner the night before. Maybe I hadn't had any sleep because Mom and Bill kept us awake all night drinking and fighting. Maybe Bill had beaten Mom black and blue. Maybe I was worried about one of my brothers or little sister who was severely abused by a drunk who wanted to feel important.

Sometimes when you know you will be going home to so many other problems you have no way to control, you feel helpless, hopeless, and lost. I truly believe a child cannot concentrate on a page of arithmetic under these circumstances. In those cases, a child runs only on survival mode.

Also, there's the fear of being made fun of by the other students, teased because you don't know the answer or because you can't spell or can't read. A child knows that the others are always watching. They see the dirty clothes, how unkempt you are; they know that no one loves or cares about you. They say hurtful, mean things to you, and everyone laughs. You feel like a bug, and you feel like some of the kids would like to step on you.

I would show all of them. I would learn to hide every weakness. No one would be permitted to see my faults. I learned if I kept quiet and listened, no one would know how smart I was or how little I knew. I practiced keeping quiet, listening and observing everything.

The children's home did not allow us to bring our books home from school. I would study my spelling words for a long time at school and then still misspell every word on the test.

Another school year was over, and it was our summer vacation. All the children were at the home all the time. It was a busy time because everyone worked. Extra staff was hired to supervise the children working. The staff did not do physical labor. I guess the strictest and the meanest staff made the best employees.

Summer break was a time when everything had to be cleaned, organized, and washed. All the wooden blinds for the numerous windows, all windows, walls, porches—everything had to be cleaned.

The older girls and boys would go with Mr. G. every morning at daybreak to his farm. He had a huge farm, and the older children at the home did all the work for him.

One Sunday, a man and woman came to the home for the lineup of children. There were not a lot of boys to choose from since most of them were working for Mr. Gr. That night at dinner, I sat with my back to the boys' table as usual. At bedtime when I went upstairs, Freddie's bed was stripped. He was gone. I didn't even get to say good-bye to the only brother I had left. I would miss him so much. At bedtime I always left him things under his blanket—little things like candy or maybe something I stole from the kitchen or something from school. They were little gifts to let him know I still cared.

Meigs County Children's Home – *Back of Home that shows the white top floor that was referred to as the 'Third Floor' where all the used clothes that had been donated. It was our store.*

Meigs County Children's Home- *Staircase to the third floor where we shopped for clothing that had been donated.*

Chapter 10
ONLY ONE ... ME

What would I do now? I needed something—something to be part of to make me whole. There was nothing left of me that had existed a couple of years ago.

Now there was only *one ... me*!

The old Erma was gone. There was only a shell of her remaining. I had a plug deep inside me, and sometimes late at night I would have a lump in my throat and tears in my eyes, but I never made a sound.

Freddie, Jimmy, Jeannie, and Bobby were gone. I saw that look they gave me whenever they were scared—the look that asked me, what should we do? I wanted to die, to never wake up again. The pain was much more unbearable than any physical pain I had ever known.

I could fix all of this under the porch. I could help the new Erma. I could make her stronger. That Erma had to remain a secret from everyone. It was just one more secret for a little girl to keep.

As I write this, I can't help but think what a strange story this is. I was safe, had three meals a day, a warm clean bed and clean clothes, but these things were nothing to me. I knew physically I was okay. I watched from far away. I was walking, talking, and going through my daily routine. Things were happening in my mind that scared me. I would be sitting in class and I didn't remember the ride to school or going to class.

I questioned if I would become like some of the children at the home. Like Helen, who stayed at the home until she was twenty-one and then moved to a nursing home. Helen acted like a child, and her top lip was funny. Everyone called her "hair lip." Maybe she had the right idea. She will never be responsible for anyone or anything. I think sometimes maybe that's not so bad.

I was alone and in so much pain. I wanted to stay in bed forever, sleeping, thinking, sleeping and thinking. I was scared and felt my only hope was the new Erma. The new Erma would become stronger, much stronger, and she did. As make-believe Erma got stronger, the real Erma became weaker. I was fading, ceasing to exist. There was nothing left of the old Erma.

I wanted to be left alone. I hated working with the smaller children. I didn't want to play games with the other children. Every bit of energy was drained from me. I had nothing left. I could do my job, but just my job. I did not want to talk with anyone or interact with anyone in any way. I wanted to be left alone. My make-believe world was becoming something different and very powerful. It was taking over my mind. I don't know how long these feelings were with me.

I remember Barbara took me in her office to talk with me. She told me Mrs. G. was worried about me. Barbara asked if something was wrong. Of course, I again lied and told her no. I had been trained long ago to say no to all questions. Were you abused? No. Are you hungry? No. Did he touch you? No. I learned my lessons well. No one would ever know how I felt. No one would ever know what my true answers were—no one.

The very next day, I got jerked back to reality. One of my teachers said, "Erma, when the bell rings, stay in your seat. I want to talk to you." He was an older man with gray hair. He seemed very old to me, maybe sixty or so.

The bell rang and I remained in my seat. He came over to me and started asking questions. His first was, "What's going on with you?" I had no answer. He wanted to know if I was in the correct grade. I didn't know where I should be. He asked if I passed the fifth grade. I told him I had never passed a grade in school. He said, "You sit here all day, but your mind is somewhere else. You never hand in any work. Your writing looks like chicken scratches." I just looked at him. I had no answers.

The teacher picked up a book and asked me to read. I tried, but I couldn't. I did know a few little words like *go*, *see*, *the*, and *me*. I told him we had moved often and that I didn't go to any school at the beginning or at the end of the school year. He told me he had searched for my school records but couldn't find any. I told him I thought I might have gone to Racine for a little while but I wasn't sure. The teacher said I couldn't read and he knew I couldn't spell or do arithmetic. He knew all of this from the few papers I had turned in. He let me go to recess.

The next day when I got to school, my teacher had a different desk for me. I sat in the back of the class, last row, the last seat on the left. I had different books and different paper.

The gray haired man told me he was a teacher and he was going to teach me. He said I would be staying in every recess and half of my lunchtime. He said the only room I would be in was his classroom. He said I would not be changing classes, which was fine with me because I had trouble changing rooms anyway. I usually got lost and ended up in the wrong room.

I had different spelling words than the rest of the class. I only had to learn five words at a time. I had flash cards for arithmetic and only one paper with problems to complete each day. Anytime any of the other students completed their assignments, they would give me my spelling words or I would read to them and they would help me.

Sometimes he would ask if anyone wanted to help me, and many students raised their hands. They really wanted to help me. My teacher told them that I had some family problems and needed everyone's help. The other children seemed happy to help me, and I learned more in that one school year than I did in my college years. My teacher really taught me that year.

At the end of the school year, he called me to his desk. He said, "Erma, if you keep working hard, you'll be okay. Learning will always be hard for you. You have a couple of wires crossed in your brain, but with hard work, you can learn. You will never be a great scholar, but you are smart and pretty, so you will be okay. You can be anything you really want to be."

My teacher and school took my mind off my make-believe family. This was one of the best things that could have happened to me. It was what I needed. I couldn't daydream in class anymore. He would walk past my desk and tell me to get to work. My teacher and school helped me to put my life in focus again. It was winter, and my times under the porch were fewer. I began picking times when I would be with my make-believe family.

One of my favorite things to do at this time was to get under my bed and lie on my back. My bedspread hung to the floor, and no one could see under the bed. No one bothered me, and they didn't know where I was.

Barbara started talking to me about going to a foster home. Mr. And Mrs. G. never seemed to mind that I didn't line up for the visitors. I really believed they wanted me to stay and take care of the little children.

I had it in my head that I would not go to a foster home, but Barbara said there would be three couples looking for a child on Sunday and she wanted me to line up. I decided to run away. I would go to Pap's and Aunt Mary's, and I would walk there.

Friday morning, I rode the bus to school, got off the bus at school, and started walking down the road. I was in Pomeroy, and I was going to walk to Letart Falls, then to Fairview where Aunt Mary and Pap lived. I walked all day, and I was very sorry when I arrived at Aunt Mary's and Pap's. Grandma was standing outside when I arrived and told me to go away. She had a crazy look in her eyes.

Aunt Mary came to the door and asked, "Where the hell did you come from?" She then said, "And you can go right back," before I had a chance to say anything. That was my Aunt Mary. She had always hated the very sight of me, and she never lost an opportunity to show me her feelings.

I remember a long time ago during one of Aunt Mary's bad moods she looked at me and said, "I hate your hair." She got up, grabbed me by the hair, and cut the front of my hair at the scalp. The children at school thought that was funny and enjoyed laughing about it for a long time. I had the same light orange hair as my Pap, and I guess this bothered Aunt Mary. Maybe, Mom always knew how Aunt Mary would treat me every time Mom dropped me off and left for months at a time. This may have been Mom's little joke on Aunt Mary and me.

Pap was outside cutting wood. He told Aunt Mary and Grandma that I could stay if I wanted to stay. He walked me into the house. The house was rundown, and I knew they were very poor.

I saw something against the wall, but I couldn't be sure what it was standing so still and flat. I had to adjust my eyes to the darkness of the inside of the house. I blinked several times and looked again.

There was a little girl standing very still against the wall. Her hair was white, and her skin was so fair. It was almost like you could see through her. She was only wearing a pair of old underwear. The little girl was all white except for her large dark eyes. She was watching everyone and everything in the room. You could see her eyes move if you watched her closely. She continued standing against the wall not moving, almost like she thought no could see her. You had to watch carefully, or she would disappear from view.

I remember thinking, *why doesn't she sit down?* After I was there for a while, I realized she always stood in a corner or off to the side. She was always out of the normal flow of the house, and you could lose her if you didn't watch her closely. After everyone was seated or settled somewhere and there was no movement, she would slide to the floor or another corner out of the way.

The little girl's name was Susie and she was my half sister. We later developed a very close relationship. Together, we have fought to have a normal life for ourselves and our children. I have three children, and Susie has four. All our children were raised in Kentucky where we found refuge.

I soon understood that Aunt Mary did not like her and treated her the same way she had treated me when I was little. Aunt Mary hated this little girl. This little girl was her only daughter, an almost unseen child.

My first evening at Aunt Mary's and Pap's , Barbara appeared and wanted me to return with her to the Children's Home. Pap walked over to her, I got behind him, and he told Barbara I was his daughter, and he would take care of me. Those were the words I wanted to hear and Barbara left.

I stayed with Aunt Mary and Pap for a couple of months until Aunt Mary took me aside and told me that my mom was in Columbus, Ohio. She said Mom had no money and some man had beaten her badly and she had to go to the hospital for a while. Aunt Mary told me that Mom wanted to come stay with her as soon as she could get there.

Aunt Mary gave me fifty cents and told me I had to go back to the children's home. She said Mom would go to jail forever if she was caught anywhere near her children. She said I had to go to protect Mom. She asked me never to tell anyone about what she said and why I left. I never did tell until now. The next morning, I got up and started walking back to the children's home. It was a very long walk. I arrived there late in the evening.

Mr. G. took his belt off and gave me a long, hard whipping and three days in isolation. This was his policy for runaways. I had to stay in the sick room. They used that room as the isolation room. I could not go downstairs to eat while in seclusion. My food was brought to me at mealtime. I didn't mind being in a room by myself. It gave me time to think about my life and my make-believe family. I could easily slip away into my make-believe world.

My bottom was sore, and it hurt to sit. My hand was black and blue from putting it behind me to try and protect my butt from the belt. It hurt to move my fingers. My arm was black and blue where Mr. G. held me so long and so tightly.

During my time in seclusion, I began thinking about my mom again. I now knew for a fact that Mom was alive. Aunt Mary had told me so. I knew if I were older I could take care of her. I decided when I got older I would get a job and buy a house for Mom and me. My mom would have a good life because I would see to it she had everything she needed. My mom would never need another old man again. She would have me, and I would take care of her. This was my dream for the next few years. I would take care of my mother and save her from any and all problems. My mother would love me.

My make-believe family was my life now. I went to them when the sadness became unbearable. The sad feelings came often, and all I wanted was to stay in bed. I wanted the real world to go away.

Eventually I learned that I could not dwell in sadness, and I began using my make-believe family to take me away from this dark place. I dreamed of family experiences like going to the movies and eating out at a nice restaurant. Sometimes Mary Jane would make me a beautiful dress and tell me wonderful stories.

Even when I was sad, I had to continue with my regular routine and responsibilities at the home. As I did what was expected of me, I felt drained of all energy. I would try not to think about anything and sleep as much as I could. I'm not sure why that sadness came and went so often. But when it came, it would stay for a long time, draining me completely of all energy.

Now I wonder if those bouts of depression had anything to do with my becoming a teenager. I also wonder why I did not have feelings of jealousy, anger, or hate. They were not a part of my feelings. Looking back now, I think my self-esteem was so low that everyone and everything seemed better than me. There were so many children filled with hate and anger, and they acted on those feelings.

Chapter 11
FOSTER CARE—EYES WIDE OPEN

One day, when I was around thirteen, Barbara called me to her office. She told me that the family who had adopted Jeannie and Bobby wanted me to come to their house for a week during the summer. I wanted to do this. I wanted to see my little sister and brother.

I had a problem—my porch family. Before, when I was away, I couldn't wait to get back to my porch family.

I reached an important decision. I would go to see my little sister and brother and I would take my porch family with me—house and all. I know this does not make any sense, but it did to me at the time.

The family that adopted my little sister and brother were good people, but it wasn't a happy home. Jeannie and Bobby looked great and were much older. Jeannie was about four and Bobby about two years old. They didn't know me, and I no longer knew them. That was sad to me. Jeannie could walk, and her back seemed okay. Bobby was beautiful. He had blond hair and the prettiest big blue eyes. At the end of the week, the family asked me to stay with them and go to school. I decided to stay. It was okay because I had my make-believe family with me. I could be with them anytime.

In the beginning, I hated hearing the stories that family told over and over about my family. They would question me often about my mom and Bill. The foster mother had friends who would visit often, and she would tell them the same stories about my family every time. She talked about when the police came and Bobby was so sick. She talked about how sick Jeannie was when the

60

police came. She would show them how thin Jeannie's hair was because of her illnesses. She would show them how Jeannie's teeth had formed wrong. She talked about my family horribly and made my mom sound like an animal. I felt it was very mean of her to talk about my family and my mom like this to all her visitors. I felt ashamed and sad when she would have Jeannie come out so she could show people her teeth and hair.

The family owned a small store, and the lady worked in it seven days a week. I took care of Jeannie and Bobby while she worked. Her husband built houses. I ended my time with this family by running back to the children's home. I gladly went back for my whipping and for my three days of isolation. I was okay with those consequences. I wanted to be far away from this foster home. I was leaving Jeannie and Bobby, but I had lost them before. I was changed and not becoming emotionally attached to anyone at this point in my life.

I came back smarter and better equipped to survive. I could lie to anyone about anything at anytime. I manipulated to get what I needed, what I wanted, or to get myself out of trouble. I looked like a young lady. I had long hair and green eyes. I looked good and I knew it. I had learned how to put makeup on, and the boys and men took notice. I would walk by, and sometimes they would whistle.

The next few years were marked by a series of foster homes and running away. I was becoming more aware and in touch with my environment. I remember one time while at a foster home I looked up and saw the moon and stars. The beauty of it took my breath away. I thought it was so wonderful. I made it a point every night to take a moment to look at the sky.

Everything seemed new to me. As the things that put us in danger seem to go away, it gives us more room for other things like learning and really feeling life. It seemed like a heavy fog was lifting and I was beginning to see things more clearly. I began to understand people better, especially foster parents.

I know there are good foster parents who foster children because they really want to be a parent and give a child a good home. They really want to make a difference in a sad child's life. They want to spend their time and money on a child who may never give them anything in return. They take in a child who only knows distrust. They take this chance with the hope and prayer they can make a difference, and sometimes they do. God bless these people. They are the very few, but they are out there.

When you take something that is broken, you spend a lot of time working on repairing the broken parts. Sometimes the broken part is too broken, or maybe a part is missing and cannot be replaced no matter how hard you try to find it. Sometimes you can fix it, and sometimes you can't. It's like the lottery. The winning tickets are few and far between. We must remember there are winners. Some foster parents take children to help them and make them a part of their family.

To me, the rest of the foster homes needed or wanted something from the children they chose. They would need workers or the money or other needs fulfilled. I can remember being told over and over in many different homes, "I'm putting a roof over your head and feeding you." They did not understand that a child *deserves* to have a warm, clean bed and food to eat.

I went to one foster home with such a large yard to mow that by the time I finished it was time to start over. They even had a pond that had to be mowed around. All the mowing was done with a push mower, kid powered. No gas-powered engines for us to use. Yes, many families wanted more than they were willing to give or do. I'm not going into all the details of the foster homes where I was sent to live. I'm sure you can correctly guess many of my unpleasant experiences. I'll just say I never did have a good foster home—or maybe I was not a good candidate for a foster home. I did come with a lot of emotional baggage. I still had my make-believe family, and I spent a little time with them each day. In my sad and unhappy times, I would stay with them more often and for longer periods of time.

During this time, I was still making plans to be with my mother. My mind was busy thinking of jobs for me and possible locations for our future home. Mom would have a wonderful new home, and I would take care of her. She would love me so much. It would just be Mom and me. We would be so happy.

I decided I wasn't going to any more foster homes, and I told that to Barbara. She said it was okay with her. She said it would give some of the other children a chance to go into foster care and maybe they would appreciate the opportunity. I was fifteen years old.

Chapter 12
MY PLAN IN MOTION

I didn't have to line up anymore. I would run away from the home only one more time. It would be my last trip. I would never return to the children's home. I would find my mother, and we would live happily ever after.

Everything about me was a lie. My make-believe family that no one knew anything about. My plans to run away, find my mother, and have a home of our own. I was still onstage and performing excellently.

School was very hard, but I managed to work through the days. The children's home did not worry about my education. They just didn't want me to cause any problems.

The children's home required that I stay out of trouble—I could do this. I could do anything to keep people happy. I wanted them to give me my space and let me be alone as much as possible. I always gave a top performance. I could do this. I was a master of manipulation. I studied people. I knew what they wanted, and I learned to tell them exactly what they wanted to hear.

I could dance around the other children at the home. Everyone liked me. I had learned at a young age to listen to what people were saying and to what they were not saying. I could manipulate other people to talk about their lives. This was important because they couldn't pry into my world while talking about themselves. This was also important to me because there was nothing in my world I could talk about.

I was Mrs. G.'s personal helper again. I handed out supplies and took care of handing out the clothes. I decided when someone else's clothes were worn or damaged. I chose the replacements. I took care of the little children and never had any other jobs to do. I could unlock the third-floor door and fold clothes or sort sizes anytime I wanted. I was being treated almost like an adult or staff member.

Mrs. G. and I talked often. I told her how kind she was and how much I loved being at the home. I told her I wanted to stay at the home and never go to another foster home. She told me when I finished school I might think about getting a job at the children's home. I could be a staff member. She had no idea about my real future plans.

I was getting ready to turn seventeen years old. School was starting in September, and I would be seventeen on October 8th. I picked the night I would run away. It would be on a weekend when Mr. and Mrs. G. were gone. I would leave after everyone had fallen asleep. I had to prepare for my escape. The door had to be left unlocked. I had to have clothes hidden under my pajamas. I had already gathered the little bit of food I would need for my journey.

I was nervous at bedtime. I had to wait for the lights to go out and then for everyone to fall asleep. We did not have a clock in the dorm, so I waited for a long time. Finally I could tell everyone in my dorm was asleep. I slid out of my bed and got the things out from under my bed for my trip. I went to the door, and the blower kicked on; I almost jumped out of my skin. The noise was a good thing. I could open the door while the blower was making this noise.

When I got outside, I knew what part of the yard I needed to cross and where I would go down the hill to get on the road. I was in for a big surprise! Sometime after my last run and before this run, someone had cut the side of the hill off, leaving a cliff with a straight drop down. I went off the cliff, tumbling down to the road far below. I thought I was dead. I lost all my survival items. I was scratched and cut up badly, and my entire body ached. My ankle was twisted, and I couldn't put any weight on that leg. Down the road a little way was a cemetery and I needed to get there. I had to follow through with my plan at any cost.

What a strange thing to happen on my first night of freedom. Who would have thought that half a hill would be missing? How could this happen? How could half a hill disappear? I had always used the same route when I ran. How could I not be aware of a hill being moved in our own backyard? My ankle was screaming in pain. I picked up a stick and used it for support. I hurt all over; my body ached. I needed to lie down for a while. When I got to the cemetery, I found a big monument and lay behind it.

I could not go another step. It was getting daylight. I slept most of the day and ached all over when I woke up. I stayed in the cemetery all that day. I was very hungry, but I knew I couldn't walk on my foot, so I stayed behind the big monument.

The next day, a woman came with flowers, and she had a small child with her. It was then that I realized I had been staying in a cemetery with dead people. That thought was a little scary.

I had to move on. I told the woman that I had to get home because my mom would be looking for me. I asked her to give me a ride. She asked me why I was in a cemetery, and I told her that I had run away and fallen down a hill. She told me how dangerous it was for a young girl to run away. She said she would take me most of the way. She took me from Pomeroy to Letart Falls, and I hobbled the rest of the way. It took me a long time to get where I was going. It hurt every step of the way.

I arrived at Aunt Mary's and was given my usual greeting. They didn't want me. I told Aunt Mary I was looking for Mom. Grandma told me that she lived just up the road. Aunt Mary told me Mom was living there now but that she was going to Columbus when she got her check. I left for Mom's house.

It was almost dark, the front door was opened, and I could tell Mom had been drinking for some time. When I walked in, she asked what was I doing there. I told her I was grown and I wanted to be with her. She didn't say anything. I told her I would work and help her with money. Mom said she only had a small check to live on and it came from her baby's father who had died. She showed no emotion.

I looked around and there was a little boy. He was the prettiest child I ever saw, with black hair and big black eyes. He had long eyelashes that curled upward. He didn't smile. He just looked at me and watched. I realized Mom had another baby. I had another little brother and he was beautiful. Mom hadn't told me to go away. She had not yelled at me, and she didn't seem angry.

In my dreams, Mom was happy to see me. She hugged me so tight. She kissed me and told me we would have a home together.

My plan could still work—only it wouldn't just be the two of us. We would also have a little boy. The three of us would have a happy home.

Mom didn't say anything about me being all dirty, skinned up, and hopping on one foot. I don't think she noticed. That was okay. I could take care of myself. I was very hungry. I asked Mom if she had anything to eat, and she told me I could eat whatever I found. I looked and found some peanut butter and bread, and I drank some water. My little brother did not speak to me, and I did not speak to him. I went to bed on the couch. I was exhausted.

Early the next morning, Barbara showed up. She asked Mom if I was there, and Mom told her yes. Mom told Barbara she had nothing to do with me being there and she wanted no trouble.

Barbara talked to Mom and told her they were releasing me from state care. Barbara felt they had done all they could do to help me. Mom told Barbara I had always been a problem but that she would keep me if the state would pay her money to do so. Barbara said no. She said the state was releasing me from their custody and I was free.

Mom got upset and told Barbara that it was just like the state to take her kid and mess up her life and then expect her to take the child back and refuse to pay her for keeping that kid. Barbara left and drove away.

I wasn't sure that Mom wanted me, but she wasn't saying she hated me or being mean. I could still make my plan work. All I had to do was get a job and show her I could take care of her. I sure wished I had some clean clothes.

Barbara came back that afternoon with my clothes, some food, and some money. Barbara cried when she told me good-bye. She told me she was sorry but it seemed I had to do things my way. She wished me luck and told me she would always be in Pomeroy. I could call her anytime and she would help me, not as a state worker but as my friend. She left me and drove away. Barbara had given me fifty dollars. I had never seen so much money. I gave Mom the money, and she was very happy. She said we were going to Columbus.

I asked Mom how we were going to get to Columbus since she didn't drive or have a car. She told me we would hitchhike. I showed Mom my swollen, black and blue ankle. I told her I had fallen off a cliff. Mom said it would be okay—that sometimes her ankles swelled too.

When Barbara was there, she had noticed all my cuts, scratches, and bruises. She asked me if someone had hurt me or beaten me up. I told her they had taken half the hill off and I had fallen off the cliff. Barbara just shook her head.

Mom had only three beers left from the night before. She drank those and started getting ready to go to Columbus. She said we would take the little boy with us. She said Aunt Mary's son, David, was mean to her little boy.

I walked over to him, and he put his arms around me. I fell in love with the tiny stranger. He didn't leave my side from that time on. I could tell that Mom didn't show him any love. She didn't hug him, hold him, or kiss him, but she wasn't mean to him. I could tell that she loved him in her way, if Mom could love anyone. I didn't admit it to myself, but I could not tell if Mom loved me.

Just before we left, Barbara pulled into the driveway again. It was her third trip from Pomeroy to Fairview that day. She brought an ace bandage, antibiotic cream, and Band-Aids for my wounds. She also brought me personal items, a toothbrush, toothpaste, deodorant, pads, and hand lotion.

I told Barbara that Mom was taking her son and me to Columbus with her. Barbara asked how we were going to get there, and I told her we were going to hitchhike. Barbara drove us to Pomeroy and bought all three of us a bus ticket to Columbus. She gave me her phone number and told me she loved me. What a strange thing and a strange feeling. No one had ever told me they loved me in my entire life. I felt like I was losing something important.

(Above and right) The Hill located off the side yard of the Children's Home- *The last time I ran away where I hurt my ankle and was hurt all over my body from the fall.*

Beech Grove Cemetery Across The Road from Children's Home- *I would run away from the Children's Home to this Cemetery where Barbara would find me.*

Beech Grove Cemetery – *I always slept behind this tombstone since it was the biggest at the time.*

Chapter 13
REUNITED AND MOVING

My trip to Columbus with Mom and my little half-brother was fun. I decided that at times my mom could be fun to be around. At the bus station, she got a taxi to take us to downtown Columbus, to Main Street. Mom was looking for a room over a bar.

She didn't find one, so Mom decided we would go to her sister's house. She lived on Vine Street that was one block off Main Street. Aunt Claudine was one of the strangest women I had ever seen. I could tell at a glance that she did not like Mom. Claudine was married to a man named John. They had two teen daughters and one son. I never met the son because he wasn't home at that time.

The girls were getting dressed to go out. Mom wanted me to go with them, but I didn't want to go, so I stayed there with my little brother. It was a good thing I didn't go; I found out later that the girls were much more experienced than I was and stayed out most nights.

John told Mom he would take her to find a room for us, and Aunt Claudine looked at Mom like she hated her. I stayed at Claudine's with my little brother. Mom and John were gone a long time. They returned and had found us a room similar to where we once lived. It seemed we always lived over a bar. We had one room with a bath down the hall. It was on a corner of Main Street. My little brother and I stayed in the room and Mom went out.

Somewhere I could hear a man and a woman fighting. I could hear things breaking and them screaming and yelling horrible things at each other.

I realized at this time that I didn't know anything. In the next two days, I came to the conclusion that I was going to get hurt there. I had felt so smart. I thought I could outsmart anyone. I could lie, manipulate, and come out a winner. I thought I knew people but I didn't know anything.

It was like Bill from my childhood had multiplied. The men looked at me like they couldn't wait to get their hands on me. *What had I done?* Every time I left our room with Mom I couldn't wait to get back home, take my little brother, and get behind our locked door.

Mom went out every night. I was afraid to go down the hall to the bathroom so I peed in a jar. I would pour it down the sink and wash the sink clean. I felt safer when Mom was there.

Mom's check and the fifty dollars Barbara had given me were soon gone. Mom started hating me again. She screamed at me. She kept reminding me that I had said I would get a job. She wanted to know what we were going to do now. Her eyes showed her hatred for me.

Mom left my little brother and me and was gone for two days. She came back with Uncle John, Aunt Claudine's husband, and they had money and food. John kissed her good-bye.

Mom was drinking, and something strange was going on with her. I was scared of her. There were times when she was talking out of her head, not from being drunk but from being crazy. She would see things that I couldn't see. She would scream at them to get away from her. Something was happening to my mother, but what?

One day I went job hunting, but I didn't have any luck. They wanted my social security number and proof of age. I had no documents. I came home and Mom had a man in the room with her and she had really been drinking. The man switched his attention to me and wanted to know if I wanted to go for a ride with him. Mom was furious. She told him to get out and pushed him. Next, she turned on me, all the hate and anger inside her directed at me.

She told me I didn't count. The only ones that counted were her and the baby. She said I was nobody. He was sitting quietly on the bed. He also knew when to get out of Mom's way. Mom said, "Who do you think you are with your uppity ways? You act like you're too good to talk and be with other people." She told me to get out. I backed out of the door. She slammed it in my face.

The day Mom told me to get out, we had already eaten all the food Mom and John had brought home. My little brother still had some milk left. He still took a bottle. I was so hungry. I could tell I had lost weight because my jeans were big on me.

I walked and walked. What would I do? I wondered if I talked to God, would he help me? I didn't think so. I had done so much wrong—lying, stealing, and manipulating others at the home. What was I going to do?

I had serious problems with the stoplights in Columbus. I did not understand the red and green of the lights. I would start walking, and the drivers would blow their horns at me and yell and show me the finger.

Chapter 14
FRANK, ANOTHER GUARDIAN ANGEL

I couldn't comprehend the logic of crossing the street when the stoplights were green or red. I had always be taught that red was stop and green was go. I needed to cross the street to get to the other side, but people would blow their horn when the light turned green and I stepped out to cross. I was afraid to walk. I had to wait and see what the cars did before I walked. Just then, the biggest truck pulled up to the corner. It was a semi with eighteen wheels. I stood back and looked up. The man behind the wheel smiled at me. I thought his smile was beautiful, like a pot of gold at the end of a rainbow. I later realized he had a gold tooth.

What a wonderful person He opened the door and I climbed onto the seat beside him. He had to give me his hand to help me up because the truck was so far from the ground. He asked me if I wanted a ride. I nodded my head yes. The problem was I didn't know where I was going. He said I could ride with him for a while. I nodded my head okay.

It was the last part of September and I would be seventeen years old in October. I told him I was eighteen. He told me he was twenty-nine. He asked if I wanted something to eat. I nodded my head yes. We stopped, and I got chili and a coke. He got a plate lunch with coffee. I decided I loved him. I knew God had sent him to me. He was the answer to my prayer.

He parked his truck, having finished his work for the night, and we got in his car. It was long and black. I thought it was the prettiest car I had ever seen. Frank said he would take me home in the car. I told him to let me out

74

on Main Street. He asked me if I would go out with him Friday night. I said yes. He didn't try to kiss me or anything.

I got out of the car knowing I would have to go back to the room where Mom and my little brother were. Frank wanted to walk me to the door, but I told him no. He waited until I was inside and then drove away. I tried the door handle and it opened, so I went inside. Mom was passed out on the bed. My little brother was playing on the floor. I picked him up, and we curled up together and went to sleep.

The next day Mom acted like she didn't remember what had happened the night before. Another thing about drunks—you never know what they will do or how they will act.

I didn't tell Mom anything about Frank. Friday night came, and Mom got dressed and went out. Frank came to the door and knocked. I did not answer because I was with my little brother. Frank went away. I was so sad I wanted to cry. About an hour later, Frank came back to the door, and I opened it. I told him I couldn't go because I had to take care of my little brother. He asked if my brother was my child, and I told him he was my brother.

Frank took us out to eat and for a drive around town. We just drove around and talked with my brother in the middle. Every time Frank would put his hand close to me, my brother would move his hand away from me. Frank and I laughed about that. My little brother did not think any of it was funny.

Frank asked me out for the next night. I told him I didn't know because everything depended on what Mom did. She might go out again unexpectedly. Frank said my brother could come with us. I really did want to go out with him again and I did feel safe with my little protector, so I agreed to go out again.

It was the end of October, the beginning of November, and Frank was coming by whenever he got off work, around 9 PM. One night he asked me to marry him, and I nodded my head yes. Frank reached out to kiss me, but I pulled away from him. He told me I needed to stop pulling away if I was going to be his wife.

I knew I would have to stop pulling away and that it was going to be difficult for me. Pulling away was an automatic response for me. I would have to work on a plan to allow him to touch me without pulling away. I began paying close attention when we were together. I noticed if I touched a part of him—his arm or hand—I could let him touch me or kiss me without jerking away. I knew this was going to take a long time to perfect.

Frank and I went to get our marriage license. We discovered that I had to have a birth certificate or have my mother sign for me to get married. I had to tell Frank I was only seventeen years old. He said he still wanted to marry me. Frank gave me twenty dollars to buy a dress for my wedding. I told Mom if she would sign at the courthouse giving me permission to marry Frank, I would give her twenty dollars. Mom said okay. I knew she would do it for money.

The ride to the courthouse was the first time Frank met my mother. We completed the trip to the courthouse and returned Mom to her room. Frank looked at me and said, "Promise me you will never look or act like her." That was a promise I had already made to myself.

The next day, we had our blood tests. We set a wedding date for December 14. Frank said he wanted us to marry before December 31 so he could claim me on his taxes.

I remember sitting in the car deep in thought. Frank was pumping gas, checking the oil and cleaning the windshield. I wondered if Frank would want to marry me if he could see inside me. Would seeing all the scars and emptiness make him change his mind? Would all the damage to my mind, heart, and soul make a difference to him?

I wondered what a wife did. I knew Mom was not an example of a wife. I didn't have a clue of what would be expected, and I had no example to go by. Every foster home I had been in was different. It seemed none of them were happy, and each wife behaved differently.

Then there was my make-believe family. I still needed time to be with them. I could never leave them. I loved them, and they loved me. I loved my time with them so much. The truth was, with them I would never have to grow up. I loved going away to the little white house with the two cars and all the love any person could ever want or need.

Did I have any clue what I was doing, and did I really want to get married to Frank? After our marriage, would Frank change? Would he hit me like I had seen Mom beaten so many times by some of her men?

The only person I could talk to and ask questions of was myself. I had no one else to talk to and no examples to follow. I did love him and I would marry him. He would take care of me, and I would try to be a good wife for Frank. Whatever a good wife was supposed to be, I would try to be the best.

Frank asked me where I wanted to get married. I told him there was a little church outside of Pomeroy. This was the church I went to with Brenda and her daughter, Mary, when we lived on Bowman's Run a long time before.

Frank said we would go on Saturday. He had to work four hours on Saturday but would pick me up at noon. At noon on Saturday, Frank did not show. He was still in his work clothes when he came to get me at 1:30. He had to work longer than he thought.

We went to Frank's apartment while he showered and got dressed. He asked me to shine his shoes while he was in the shower. I had never done that before, but I tried. I put a lot of polish on his shoes, too much polish. It took Frank a long time to get it off and fix the mess I had made of his shoes.

Frank was rushed, tired, and irritable. It was quickly becoming a bad day. It had begun raining, and we hadn't eaten. Frank decided we would eat when we got to Pomeroy.

We arrived in Pomeroy after 6 PM. We stopped at a phone booth, and Frank asked me to call the church. No one answered the phone. Frank decided to drive to the church. On our way, I realized I had left my purse in the phone booth. I hated telling Frank, but I had to because our marriage license was inside. He turned around and drove back to the phone booth. He never said a word. Luckily my purse was still there in the booth. I guess no one had used the phone because of the pouring rain. I wanted to cry. It had been a long time since anyone had seen me cry and it wasn't going to happen tonight.

We finally arrived and no lights were on inside the church. I went to the house beside the church. It was the same minister I had seen as a little girl. He refused to marry anyone that had been married before. Frank was divorced and had two daughters.

Frank asked what should we do, and I told him we could go to Rutland to another church I had gone to as a foster child. The minister married us, and Frank gave him $20. I was wet, tired, very hungry, and married. Frank decided to drive back to Athens before we ate. We arrived in Athens after 11 PM. We had a hard time finding a place to eat because almost everything was closed for the night. Finally, we ate and then Frank got us a room for the night. He said we had to get up early to get back to Columbus to find an apartment and get our things moved.

My dream of working and getting a house and making a home for my mom was over. I believe I always knew in my heart that Mom would always choose a man over me, any time.

I was married and had no idea what was next. Would I be okay? All I knew was I had no one but this man. He was now in charge of my life. I did love Frank, but I was afraid of the rushed, irritable side of him. I did not understand this drive of his to get so much done. I had never known anyone like him before. I hoped this was a good thing.

Chapter 15
MARRIED LIFE—WHO KNEW?

Saturday, I woke up a child—maybe a dysfunctional child, but still a child. Sunday, I was expected to be an adult. I was expected to be a woman with the ability to run a house. I was supposed to have the good sense to clean a house, do laundry, prepare meals, plus the know how to shop for groceries and understand all the other wifely responsibilities. I had none of these skills. My only qualification was that I knew how to bathe small children.

The first time I had a moment to think was Monday morning after Frank went to work. I thought back to Saturday night, our first night as a married couple. I was so tired, my body was screaming for sleep. Frank gave me the talk again about not pulling away from him. Sleep would not come for me until Frank went to sleep. Thankfully it did not take long; he was exhausted.

As soon as he was asleep, I moved away from him, slowly. I had never slept close to anyone before, and I felt like I couldn't breathe. I remember thinking that I may not like married life. The only thing I knew for sure at that moment was that Frank loved me. Frank was born in Kentucky. His parents had seven children and were honest, hardworking people. They were a loving family. Two of his sisters were my age. Frank was divorced and had two beautiful daughters. I think the girls were about six or seven years old when we got married. I could tell Frank loved his little girls and wanted to be with them. It was hard for him because he worked in Columbus and had to work all the time.

Frank married a stranger. He married me and knew nothing about me or my world. I was a stranger in his world too. I did not know about cooking, cleaning, laundry, and other daily responsibilities. I knew nothing about love except for my make-believe family.

The man I married was a good person, a good man. He always worked hard and supported his family. Frank was—and still is—family oriented. He has always had goals and has always worked toward these goals.

I mostly admire Frank because he has never stopped learning new things. He never stopped trying to improve his education or his skills. He never stopped trying to become a better person.

Frank is very tenderhearted and considerate of other people's feelings. When my grandmother died, Frank cried during her services, even though he had never met her. During her last years, Grandma had become meaner; no one cried for her that day except Frank.

Frank just speaks his mind. His bluntness was difficult for me and caused me great stress. He has no tolerance for bad habits or faults. Frank's philosophy was you just need to shape up and do what's right. It was always Frank's laws and Frank's way. That caused problems from the beginning of our marriage. I never lived up to Frank's standards, and his high standards kept him from having a lot of friends.

Sunday morning, my first day of married life, I was awakened to Frank's voice saying, "We need to a get a move on." It was almost 6 AM. He asked if I wanted to shower first, so I showered, but I really just wanted to stay in bed alone. I'm sure you've noticed that I've made no mention of makeup, hair, or clothes. I had nothing with me because I could not think that far ahead. I had to put on the dress that I wore to get married. It was okay because it was a plain shirtwaist white dress.

Frank said that since it was our wedding weekend we would have a sit-down breakfast. He seemed to have so much to do, and I didn't have a clue about what we needed to do. We went to a restaurant, and Frank got the plate lunch special. I was worried because I had never eaten in a restaurant until I started dating Frank. The first time we had gone to a restaurant, the waiter said, "The chili is good," so I ate chili everywhere we went. I didn't understand things like plate meals or side dishes. Also, I had seen in a movie that there's a correct way and a wrong way to use silverware. I didn't have a clue, but I knew I couldn't order chili for breakfast. I told the waitress I wanted a fried egg sandwich. One of my foster homes had served this to us for breakfast. I made it through our wedding breakfast.

We arrived in Columbus about 11 AM. Frank was trying to find a newspaper to look for houses or apartments for rent. It would have to be furnished because we had no furniture. I had never looked at a newspaper before and became panicky when he handed it to me. I couldn't read very well, and there were so many lines of words on the paper. Frank was rushed and irritable. He seemed to be feeling a lot of pressure. He took the newspaper from me and said, "You can't do anything." I wanted to cry. What a mess.

Eventually we were calling and looking at apartments. Frank told me to use the phone booth to call about an apartment. I couldn't seem to get the numbers straight. I kept reversing the numbers when I tried to dial. I just wanted to run away.

Sunday night, we found an apartment. We then started moving Frank out of his apartment. It took four carloads to move all of Frank's clothes and other items from his apartment to our new home. We then went to get my things from Mom's room. She wasn't home and the door was unlocked. I had two small sacks of clothes and personal items. We returned with those to our apartment.

It was about ten o'clock, and I was exhausted. Frank told me we had to get to bed because he had to be on the job at 6 AM. We had not eaten since breakfast. I began to realize that food was not important to this man I had married. We ate some peanut butter with crackers and a banana before going to bed.

The next morning, Frank got up for work. He said we would go to the grocery when he got home from work. I said okay, and he went to work and I went back to bed. I slept and did not wake until about 2 PM. I finally got up and took a bath. I was emotionally and physically exhausted.

I finished my bath and sat down to wait for Frank to come home. I remember thinking that I should put my clothes away, but I didn't do it because I didn't know what drawers to use.

Frank came home around six o'clock, took a bath, and got dressed. We went to the grocery store. He kept asking me questions about what I wanted to cook. I told him I didn't know, and he looked at me like I had two heads, so I tried to think. I thought of chicken, potatoes, and bread. After I realized this was what Frank wanted me to do, I chose several food items. I forgot things like salt, oil, butter, and sugar. Toilet paper did not make it in the cart of things we needed either.

It was late when we got home, but I could tell I was expected to prepare dinner. It was hard to do this for two reasons: first, I had forgotten to get the basics (oil, etc.), and second, *I did not know how to cook*!

I just kept turning around in the kitchen trying to think of what to do. Frank asked what was wrong with me. I told him I did not know how to cook. He was stunned! He told me he had never heard of someone my age not knowing how to cook. I felt terrible, but he hugged me and said it would be okay.

Frank began looking for his clean work clothes for the next day, and he asked why I hadn't put away the clothes. I told him I wasn't sure where or how he wanted his clothes. I had not put my clothes away because I wanted Frank to have the drawers he wanted.

Frank and I had another talk. This was our second talk. The first talk was about not pulling away. The second talk was about my responsibilities. Frank told me that the clothes and the house were my responsibilities. Working and earning a living was his job. He said he wanted a hot meal when he got home from work. I was responsible for finding a Laundromat close to home to do our clothes. He told me I needed to clean the apartment.

Frank told me he loved me but it would take both of us doing our jobs to make a home. I told him the house looked clean to me. He said no, I needed to take all the dishes out and wash them. I needed to clean the bathroom. He named several things a wife was supposed to do. I decided I was going to hate being a wife.

I didn't want to learn that many things. I couldn't remember that many things. I wanted two or three things to learn and get good at. I also wanted free time to daydream, to think and be with my family. I wondered what he would do if I ran away.

One of our many problems was that Frank was not a teacher and I had so many things to learn. Frank had his own way of doing things, and he was very set in his ways. This became a problem for us.

Frank said we would be going to his parents the week between Christmas and New Year. I was scared. I would be meeting his two daughters. What if they didn't like me? I had seen many pictures of them, and they looked really nice. Their hair was very long and they had beautiful clothes.

I only had two pairs of jeans, one skirt, and the dress I had gotten married in. My tops were old but I think they looked okay. My tennis shoes were okay. Thinking back, I don't remember having any other shoes. I wonder if I got married in tennis shoes. I can't remember.

Tuesday, I put away our clothes. Frank had so many things. I felt confused. I folded all of his shirts and put them in a drawer. I used another drawer for his pants. I still had his underwear and socks to put away. I never knew anyone who needed an entire drawer for socks. What a mess! I was so overwhelmed by all the clothes. It was too much for me.

I now believe this was so difficult for me because with Mom I had no clothes. At the children's home we were allowed only five outfits and one Sunday outfit. We were not allowed extras of anything. I was in charge of one towel and one washcloth and was told where to put them. I had a place for everything I needed, nothing extra.

A house full of things is like a large dump. I can't deal with so many things. I had no place to put them away. Everything must be put away—Children Home Rules. Now I had mountains of things to put away.

I remember my first week of marriage like it was yesterday. Tuesday I folded clothes. I went back to bed after Frank left for work. I got out of bed around 2 PM. I could sleep all day. This became my daily routine. I got up with Frank, packed his lunch, and prepared his breakfast. He liked bacon, eggs, toast, and coffee for breakfast. I would go to bed as soon as I knew he was gone for the day. I got my best sleep after Frank left. I loved sleeping or lying in bed daydreaming. I guess I was spending about sixteen hours a day in bed.

Frank came home Tuesday night. I had prepared a dinner of fried chicken, potatoes, and pork-n-beans. Frank took a bite of the fried chicken and it was bloody inside. He just looked at me. I told him I thought it was done when it was browned. Frank told me to put it in the oven and let it bake and I could serve it tomorrow night.

He asked if I had washed all the dishes in the cabinets. I nodded my head yes. This was the first of many lies I would tell my husband over the next twenty-eight years.

I can't remember ever wanting to please anyone as much as I wanted Frank to be proud of me. I just could not be the wife Frank wanted, though I tried to be better and be all that he wanted me to be.

During this time, I was an emotional mess wondering if Frank would stop loving me. I continued to do things wrong like folding all his shirts and pants and putting them in the dresser drawers. This made him upset. He told me they needed to be on hangers so they wouldn't wrinkle.

I wondered if I was bad or didn't get things right, would he do what the foster homes had always done? In a foster home, if a child rebelled or refused to follow instructions, they were punished or sent back to the children's home. Only the foster parents' own children could get away with being rebellious or bad.

My first married week seemed to go by fast. It was time to go meet Frank's parents and the rest of the family. I was terrified.

I had been spending my time with my make-believe family whenever Frank was at work. I loved every minute of being with my family. I could be a little girl. Mary Jane loved me and took care of me. Everything was wonderful, and I was happy.

Frank came home from work, and we were getting ready to go to his parents. We had no clean clothes because I had not gone to the Laundromat. I had not left the apartment. I told Frank I hadn't gone because I didn't know where it was. I didn't know how to get the clothes there and I didn't have any laundry detergent to wash the clothes with. Frank just looked at me and said, "My, my." I wondered what he meant by that. It couldn't have been good. I had to do better. Poor Frank! Frank took me and our clothes to the Laundromat. It was two doors down from our apartment.

Frank showed me how to wash the clothes using the machines and how to use the dryers. He told me he would keep change in a cup and I could go whenever I needed to do laundry. We finished all the laundry and went home to bed.

We started for Booneville, Kentucky at four in the morning. I didn't want to go. In fact, I didn't even want to get out of bed. I remember thinking, *I can't live like this.*

It was difficult for me having someone so close all the time, always wanting more from me than I had to give, always trying to make me smarter and more organized. Frank was always telling me to pay attention. He had so much to do. He was busy building a life, and I was busy trying to avoid life.

On the way to Booneville, I pretended to be asleep. I was really thinking. I was going to meet his parents and his children. Would his parents look inside me and see who I really was? Would they see all the damage and emptiness? I was terrified. Would they see how dumb I really was? I didn't know anything about being a wife to Frank. His family would know this as soon as they saw me. They would know I was dirt, unworthy to be in their family.

My mother was a whore and an alcoholic, and Frank's family would know all of this when they looked at me. They might laugh at me or turn me away. I had this awful tattoo on my arm. The children at school had often made fun of my tattoo, and I hated it. I had worn a long-sleeve shirt to hide it, but I knew at some point someone would see it and tell the rest of Frank's family.

The worst that could happen would be if they found out that my mother did not and had never loved me. No one loved me. No one wanted me. I had to brace myself for what was surely to come. Would Frank turn me away too?

These thoughts brought a new line of thinking for me to focus on. Why hadn't Frank ever asked me anything about my past? I had told Frank when we met that my mom hadn't raised me and that I had stayed with an aunt most of my childhood.

Frank had never asked anything about my father or mother. He had asked nothing about my family or my life. This entire holiday week, he had never asked if I wanted to go see my mom. When we went to Pomeroy to get married, Frank asked nothing about my aunt. He asked nothing about me or my past. Nothing!

As a child, life had been hard, scary, and at times unbearable, but as an adult, life was going to be harder. I thought of Helen, the girl who went from the children's home to a nursing home. Her life sounded better to me as each of my new days went by.

It was about breakfast time when we arrived at Frank's family's home. His daughters came running out to meet him. Frank had told his daughters that he was bringing home a friend. After they hugged him, they turned to me. Frank introduced me to them and told them I was his wife. He told the girls we had gotten married ten days ago. Both girls started crying. I felt terrible. They kept holding onto their dad, crying. I just stood beside Frank. I didn't say or do anything.

I wanted to say, "That's okay, stop crying, you can have your daddy back. I really wasn't going to like married life anyway." In fact, at that moment, I wanted to leave and never return.

JoAnn, his oldest daughter, who was seven, told her daddy that she was upset because her mother told them that if their daddy got married they would not be going to Columbus to stay for holidays and summer vacation.

I discovered that the children had always done this since the divorce. During those visits, Frank's sister came to Columbus to stay with them. Frank told the girls he would go and talk to their mother and try to get her to change her mind.

All I remember thinking was, *God, please help me make it through this week.* I promised myself I would never return to Frank's parents' home again.

Frank's youngest daughter, Jackie, who was six, asked Frank where I going to sleep. Frank looked at me and said he always slept with the girls when he was at his parent's home. Frank would be sad if he knew how glad I was to hear this. *A whole week of being in a bed all by myself. Thank you, God.*

We went in the house and met Granny and his dad. Everyone called him Pa. Frank had two sisters who were about the same age as me.

Granny took me to show me where I would be sleeping. She said she hoped I didn't mind Frank sleeping with the girls while we were there. I told her that was fine with me because I really liked sleeping alone.

Granny stared at me a long time. I told her I always slept better alone, and she said I needed to get over wanting to sleep alone. She said, "Sleeping with your husband is part of being married." I thought to myself, *Good job, Erma, now Frank's mother knows you hate sleeping with your husband, her son.*

The week was very hard for me. I was seventeen years old with no social skills, no self-esteem, and no self-confidence. I had nothing to talk about. I had no answers to all of their questions. They asked lots of questions: Where did I grow up? Did my parents mind me marrying an older man? What school did I go to? What did my father do for a living? Did my mother work outside the home? Did I have any brothers and sisters? What? What? What? *God, please help me get through this week.*

I did have some fun that week playing with Frank's daughters. I told them stories, and we played Old Maid. We had a great time playing with the toys they had. After a couple of nights, they asked if they could sleep with me. I said no, that I slept better alone. JoAnn and Jackie liked to get up so early and come to my bed. They were laughing, playing, wanting to have tickle time, talk, and play games. *God, please let this week be over.*

Finally the week was over and I realized I loved everyone there. Granny was wonderful. The first morning we were there, she prepared an unbelievable breakfast. She fixed biscuits, gravy, fried potatoes, eggs, and bacon. It was a feast. I remember someone saying, "Pass the redeye gravy." They passed this dish around of water and grease. I thought it was the strangest thing I had ever seen, but when I tasted it, I loved it.

One thing I can say about that week is this was the kindest, most loving family I had ever seen. Anyone would be blessed to be in that family. Life is so strange. It keeps knocking you down, and then it hands you a special gift—a gift so wonderful you know you don't deserve it.

We went back in Columbus to our one-bedroom apartment. I remember our first day home. I walked around looking at it as if it was the first time I had seen it. Frank's parents and sisters sent loads of stuff home with us. We barely had room to sit in the car on the way home. They gave us towels, dishes, blankets, sheets, pictures to hang, whatnots, and canned food. Granny told me she wanted her jars back. Frank's sisters gave me a mountain of clothes. Frank was happy about getting all of this stuff. I wanted to cry. It was just more for me to keep organized. We only needed two plates, and we had sixteen. The cabinet was already filled with things that came with our furnished apartment.

I knew my job was the house. I had to get rid of all of this stuff before Frank got home. I piled everything I could under the bed. I filled the bottom of the only closet we had.

I still had boxes of clothes his sisters had given me. I picked out two dresses, two pairs of pants, two tops, and one pair of shoes. I then took everything else and put it in the trash. In my mind, I kept thinking, *I can't tell Frank.* He was so happy about getting all of it. After I was done, I sat there and thought, *there must be something wrong with me.*

I was not normal. Our apartment was so plain. I had nothing on any of the tables or shelves. Nothing was sitting on the kitchen table. There was nothing, no woman's touch. Our apartment did not look anything like Frank's mother's home. Our apartment did not look like a home. It looked like the children's home.

I knew down deep that I was not a homemaker. I had no natural ability to make a house a home. I had never had the feel of a real home. How was I going to make a home? *Maybe it's a good thing Frank works all the time,* I thought. It would take him longer to realize I was just a shell.

I missed my Barbara. Every time I couldn't go on or I fell apart, she would take my hand. She would take me to a safe place and she would have time for me. Barbara would listen and I would have a place to put myself back together. I would have time to repair.

Frank expected so much from me, and his family expected so much. They had asked questions and expected answers. Responsibilities kept adding up.

I needed time away for myself. They were all keeping me away from my true family, my make-believe family. Soon I would no longer exist.

I needed to become an adult at seventeen, with no past or problems of my own. Nothing. I could not do this. I was a real person at seventeen, and I had a past. I was so confused and scared. I was married but felt so alone. *I am all alone. I will work this out. I will be okay, but not now, tomorrow.*

I had to take a bath, do my hair, iron Frank's shirt and pants, and prepare dinner. I needed to make sure the tub was spotlessly clean. I had to remember to lay out a towel and washcloth for him.

I would have time to think about all these things after Frank went to sleep. He always fell asleep quickly because he worked such long hard days. I wondered why he did this. I never knew anyone who worked a regular job on a daily basis. In fact, no one in my family ever worked. Maybe I was lazy. That was it, I decided. Frank had a seventeen-year-old lazy wife.

Thank God we had decided not to have any children. I was afraid I would be a mother just like my mom. No child should have to live like that, not with me as a mother like my mother.

Tomorrow I would work on my problems. I needed to get smarter. I needed to learn what a wife thinks and feels. I needed a book to read. Funny, I forgot I couldn't read well, let alone comprehend what I was reading. Anyway we didn't have any books or a television. I would work this out.

My make-believe mother could sew. She could cook and had pictures hanging on our walls. Mary Jane was the perfect wife and mother.

I would hang those pictures that Frank's mother gave us. I would unpack those flower vases and the ducks his family gave us, and I would set these things out on our tables. I could do these things. I would be a great homemaker. I would just have to work on it the way Frank worked on making a living. Somehow I would learn how to do these things.

That night when Frank came home, he told me it was time to go to

Booneville and see his girls. He visited them every few weeks. I said okay, but inside I was thinking, *No God, please, not again.*

Frank said he wanted me to stay there with his mother so I could learn how to cook and keep house. I told him I was already cooking and keeping house. Frank said that what I was doing could not be called being a homemaker or a wife. He told me I could not cook. He said our apartment was not clean and that there was much work that was not being done.

Frank pointed out several problem areas that needed a homemaker's attention. The list was long: cobwebs hung from the ceiling and in the corners, windows needed to be washed, the woodwork needed to be washed, and the porch needed to be washed. Frank said the kitchen floor should be mopped every day. Ironing should be done the same day as the laundry, not left sitting in a basket. The list went on and on as I drifted away.

I drifted far back to the past. Back to the first time I went to the Meigs County Children's Home. I don't know how old I was, but it was before I started school. I was shocked at what a gigantic place it was. The home was the biggest place I had ever seen. We walked up the steps to the huge front door. I don't believe I could have opened it by myself. I don't remember who brought me there, but they opened the door for us to go inside. We walked inside the door into a long hallway. The floor was so shiny.

I will always remember Mrs. G. entering the hallway. She had black hair and wore glasses. Her dress looked like it was stiff. I later learned that the girls at the home ironed her clothes. The dresses had to be starched and ironed until they were stiff. Should the dress not be stiff enough, the girls would have to redo it.

Mrs. G. started going down a long list of my responsibilities and the rules of the home. She said never to go upstairs because that was where the boys slept. Never talk to anyone in the hallway. I could go downstairs to the cafeteria only when the bell rang. She then walked me back to a long room with two rows of twin beds. She told me which bed was mine and told me I was not to sit on or get in anyone else's bed. The beds all looked alike, and that scared me because I knew I would never remember which bed was mine. One wall had a row of closets, maybe about twenty. She told me which one was mine. I couldn't remember that either because they all looked alike.

She gave me a paper sack. She told me to go into the bathroom and take off all my clothes and shoes and put them in the sack. She said she would give me different clothes later. She gave me a little bucket and put my name on it. Inside was soap, shampoo, and the smallest hairbrush I had ever seen. Later I learned that this was a toothbrush, and we had toothpaste also.

As she was going down the list, she looked up at me and said, "You don't menstruate?" I shook my head no. I didn't know what that was, but I was sure I didn't do it.

She started running water in the tub to show me how much water to put in the tub. She asked me if I knew how to wash my hair in the tub. I told her no. She showed me how to do this. She told me to leave the bathroom clean, and she showed me where the cleaning supplies were kept. She showed me where to put my washcloth and towel. She said the next day after washing my face, my washcloth and towel would go in a basket and someone would leave a clean set for me on my bed later.

I remember thinking that I was like a fly that gets in the house, flying around not able to remember how it got in or how to get out. If the fly lands on the wrong thing and gets smashed, just like that it's gone. The sad thing is no one cares. I wondered if flies go to heaven.

I wondered if this woman would be the one to smash me. I would never remember all the things she was telling me to do. Just like I would never remember all the things Frank was telling me to do. It seemed like one or two things were all I could handle at one time.

Frank was coming to the end of his list, and I drifted back. He was saying these were my jobs, not his. Frank said he loved cornbread and that his mother fixed cornbread every night. All I gave him was white bread and he hated white bread.

Finally he was coming to the close of our talk. He said he didn't want me to feel he didn't love me with all his heart. I just needed to learn what my responsibilities were, learn how to do them and then do them right. Then I heard Frank saying, "Erma, did you hear anything I said? Are you listening to me? I swear, I don't know how to get through to you."

Frank's solution to our problem was two weeks with his mother. Well, I had wanted to learn. *Thank you, God, for answering my prayer. Next time, I'll be much more careful about what I pray for.*

We went to Booneville, and Frank laughed as he told his mother to teach me to be a good housewife and homemaker.

The family was now bursting with more questions. Didn't my mother make me help around the house? Didn't I cook a meal once in a while? Didn't I have to keep my room clean? Hadn't I ever made fudge or brownies before? No. No. No.

The two weeks with Granny were good for me. I got up with Granny at 5:30 every morning. We milked the cow. I could do that because I had milked Nanny. We fixed a big breakfast and sometimes we baked cakes and pies.

Granny's routine was the same as far as the house duties. It ran like this: milk the cow, prepare breakfast, do dishes, sweep and mop the kitchen floor, go through the house, make the beds, sweep, dust the living room, and sweep the porch. Everything was completed by 9 AM.

We then started the work for that day, such as laundry, hoeing the garden, canning, mowing the yard, working in the fields with Pa, or catching, killing, cleaning and cooking a chicken.

One thing I know for sure, I did learn from Granny. She was a hard worker and one of the kindest people I have ever known. I learned how to cook and clean, but I wasn't sure I wanted to live like Granny. Her joy seemed to be reading the obituary column, talking to a neighbor about all the work she had done that day, or cooking a huge meal and cleaning up afterward.

Don't take this the wrong way. I loved and had the deepest respect for Granny. She was a great, loving, good Christian woman. Her joys were just not what a seventeen-year-old would consider joyous.

I would fall very short in my life story if I did not credit Granny for all the knowledge, guidance, patience, and love she gave to me. She was and still is my idea of a woman, a wife, and a mother. Most of all, I would like to say that Granny was a most precious child of God. She taught me so many things.

Granny could work all day in the garden, mowing the yard, canning, and whatever needed doing that day, and when the family gathered around the table at mealtime, it would be set with a meal fit for a king and enough food to feed an army.

How she could do all that work and still have a meal prepared has always been a mystery to me. How did she have the time? Everything she prepared came from the farm and was made from scratch.

Granny was a large woman with an angelic look about her. She had a sweet, kind face. Her whole life was doing God's work, being a mother and a wife. Granny loved her home. She always seemed to have a song in her heart and on her lips. Granny told me one time long ago, "Life can be that you have joy, but from what I've seen, it is also filled with hardships. During these times you have to pray and work harder." Granny loved her children deeply. She always tried to have a little something special for each child.

I've seen Granny's hands red, cracked, and bleeding from washing clothes outside in the wintertime. Pa would build a big fire outside, and Granny would wash their clothes outside in a tub. She would then hang them on the clothesline outside. The clothes would freeze as Granny hung them on the line. The entire time, she would be singing a hymn, and you knew she had a prayer in her heart.

Granny was my greatest example of what a woman, wife, and mother should be. She was a shining example of all three. I came home a better homemaker. I made cornbread in a little iron skillet Granny had given me, and I made it every day. I still went back to bed as soon as Frank went to work, but I did everything I needed to do when I got out of bed at noon.

A few weeks later, I decided I wanted to see Mom and my little brother. I ventured out of our apartment and got on a bus and went to Columbus. I knew Mom's sister Claudine would know where Mom was. She lived off Main Street in a rental house. She and her family had lived there for years.

I knocked, and Aunt Claudine opened the door. I asked her if she knew where my mother was. She said, "Come in and I'll tell you about your mother." We went into the living room and I sat down. When I looked over in the corner, there sat my baby brother. I started to go over to him, but he screamed at me. I asked Aunt Claudine what was wrong with him. She said Mom had dropped him off weeks ago and hadn't come back. I couldn't believe Mom would do this.

Aunt Claudine was mean and hated everything that belonged to Mom. Remember, her two daughters were prostitutes. I wondered what they were doing to my brother, but he wanted nothing to do with me. He was about two and a half years old at the time. She told me Mom still lived over the bar. I said good-bye and went to find her.

I knocked on Mom's door, and when she opened it, she looked at me with hate in her eyes. She said, "You get out of here, you little bitch. My man doesn't know I have kids." She slammed the door, and I knocked again. She wouldn't open the door, so I talked to her through it. I told her there was something wrong with my little brother and I was afraid he was being hurt.

She told me she couldn't take care of him right now and for me to stay out of her life.

I cried all the way home. I have always wished I could have done more, but I knew Frank would not let him live with us. At that point, I wasn't even sure Frank was going to keep me.

One day in May, Frank came home around 2 PM and said he had gotten in an argument with his boss and had quit his job. He asked me if I was upset about him quitting. I told him that it was entirely up to him and did not affect me.

He looked at me and said, "You just don't get it!" He said we couldn't pay our bills if he didn't have a job. Good grief! What did he want from me? He had said over and over that earning a living was his job. Now he was yelling at me because I didn't get mad at him because he had quit his job. Nobody in my family ever had a job to quit.

Frank finally settled down. He said we needed to get up at 5:30 and go to Bellefontaine, Ohio. He had worked with a company building a road between Bellefontaine and Columbus, Ohio.

The next morning, the alarm went off at 4:30. He told me to shower first. I showered and then fixed breakfast while he showered. He told me I had fifteen minutes to get the breakfast dishes done. I wondered what Frank would say if he knew I didn't do breakfast dishes until I got up at noon every day. He sure didn't know me, and he didn't seem to care. Maybe he didn't care because he thought he was developing the wife he wanted. I still had a long way to go, but I could manage as long as he worked so many hours. That gave me time—time to sleep and to be with my make-believe family. That was the only time I was happy. I did love Frank; to me, he was perfect. I just had to lie to him about who I was. Frank and I were so different. Frank had his perfect, loving family, and I had my secrets.

All of my secrets were making me an empty shell. Would I ever feel as good as other people? Would I ever have experiences to talk about with other people? I just wanted other people to see me as an equal, as a good, smart person.

Meigs County Children's Home -- *This is exactly
how I remember seeing the Home the first time
Barbara took me as a young child. It was the
BIGGEST house I had ever seen*

Meigs County Children's Home Side Door --
*Barbara always walked us around to this door
when she brought us to the home. This door
always stuck in mind as SO huge. I could not
open it by myself.*

94

Chapter 16
BELLEFONTAINE—
RESPONSIBILITIES AND MISSIONARIES

We arrived outside Bellefontaine and stopped at a temporary office set up for the workers on the new four-lane road project. Frank got out of the car. I watched him. He seemed to know exactly where to go and whom to talk to. He returned to our car and said he had to begin working immediately.

He had his work clothes in the trunk. He slipped on his coveralls and told me he was sorry but I would have to stay in the car all day because we needed this job. I asked him what to do if I needed to pee. Frank told me there was a bathroom behind the office. He left. I lay down in the seat. I was so tired, so very tired. It was just getting daylight.

Frank didn't stop working until 5:00. He came to the car and said one of the men told him where there was a place to rent. We were going to go see it. He slipped off his coveralls and went someplace to wash his face and hands. I told Frank after he got cleaned up that I really needed a drink and I was very hungry. He said we would stop and get a pop. He got one pop, and we shared it.

Frank saw the landlord when we got to the rental house. He and the landlord came downstairs and went inside the door on the first floor. Frank came out and said we would be moving there.

Frank drove us back to Columbus to our apartment. He told me to get some of my clothes. It was Tuesday, and we would come back Sunday to get of the rest of our things. We drove back to Bellefontaine that night.

Frank started his bath as soon as we had eaten something we had brought from our apartment. We had to wait to eat because we couldn't eat in Frank's car. I just wanted to go to bed. I told him I would bathe in the morning.

Frank pointed out to me that even though the apartment was furnished, we still needed to put our own sheets on the bed. So, I took their sheets off the bed and put our sheets on. I didn't even know he had packed our extra set of sheets in the box with our towels. It was 12:30 AM and we had to get up at 5:30. I almost hated him.

The next morning, he let me stay in bed. He told me he would stop and get something for breakfast on his way to work. I didn't even pack his lunch. I slept until 2 PM. I didn't want to get up then, but I had to unpack the things we brought from our apartment in Columbus. I also had to take my bath and get Frank's supper. We started our routines.

On Sunday, Frank borrowed a truck and we moved everything from Columbus to Bellefontaine in one trip. On the way back to our new apartment, Frank told me we would be going the next weekend to get his girls for their summer break. They would be staying with us. *Dear God, please just let me drop dead now. Let me die right now.*

How could I watch two little girls, cook three meals a day, clean up, and take care of everything else Frank needed me to do? What would the girls do all day? I asked Frank if he would be working, and he said yes, every day. We would drive down Saturday afternoon. Frank would work till noon. It sounded just like my wedding night. We would be coming back on Sunday.

Monday, I walked downtown. Frank didn't have time to take me to the store, and town was only a few blocks away. I walked past a store that was selling TVs. The sign said For Sale—TV, $10 a month, Pay Here. I went inside. I got a TV. They would deliver it the next day. I was hoping Frank would be okay with me buying a TV. Frank came home, and I tried to tell him about the TV all night, but I just couldn't. What was I going to do? I worried all night.

The next morning, Frank left for work. At 9 o'clock, my TV arrived, little antenna on top. It was too late, and there was no way I could hide it. I thought of saying I found it, but someone was going to have to pay that $10 every month.

Frank walked in, and I started crying. I told him I was leaving. He asked what the matter with me now was and then he saw the TV. Frank's face turned red.

He asked me what I done, and I told him I had bought a TV and it was only $10 a month. He started shouting at me. He said we didn't have any money and when we got a TV we would pay cash. Frank didn't believe in buying things on time. He always said that if you have to buy something on time, then you don't need it. He slammed the bathroom door and took his bath. I just sat on the couch. Finally he came out and said that he had thought about getting a TV for Christmas. He also said I had no right to do what I did.

I remember what I said to him just like it was yesterday: "Go to hell and take your clean car and your two little girls with you. I'll go back to the place I ran to, my graveyard. I'll live there before I'll spend another day with you. You may be perfect, but I'm not ready for a perfect husband. Good-bye." I stormed out the door and started down the street. I was scared. I intended to go to Pomeroy, and I had never walked that far before. I didn't even know if I was going in the right direction.

After walking a couple of blocks, Frank drove up in his car. He told me to get in. I stopped and looked at him. He said he was sorry and we could work this out. I got in the car and we went home. He kissed me and wanted to make love. Frank always thought this fixed everything. It did not.

The next morning, after Frank went to work, I did not go back to bed. I just sat on the couch and kept going over everything in my mind. *What do I need? What do I want?* I remembered two things I never wanted in my life: First, I never wanted to be like my mom. I knew I was not like her. I didn't drink, curse, smoke, or chase men. I would never talk mean or be physically abusive to anyone. I really tried to love everyone from a safe distance. Second, I did not want to be with anyone who drank, cursed, or was mean or dirty in any way. I wanted someone who really loved me.

I really believed Frank fit the definition of what I wanted. He didn't even smoke. I was with a hardworking, perfect man. I loved him with all my heart, but I wasn't sure I liked him.

Frank always wanted more from me than I could give. I couldn't seem to find the answers I was seeking. I had run from homes and situations my entire life. I couldn't do that this time. I needed to stay and be an adult for the first time in my life.

I wished I had someone to talk to about my problems, but I had no one. Barbara had released me from state custody, and I felt apart from her. I had no childhood friends. I didn't know any of our neighbors. I was so alone. I could go to the pay phone and make a call, but I had no one to call, no one to get advice from or to listen to me. I was on my own. I had to talk myself through this. I had to think and think until I came up with the answers. I wished Frank and I were old; then most of this lonely, hard life would be over.

I remembered one time when I had run away, Barbara said to me, "Erma, let's go back to the children's home. We'll get a good night's rest, and then we'll take one thing at a time. Things will work out." It was at a time when I wanted to go live with Aunt Mary and Pap. I guess Barbara knew that wasn't the best situation for me. Barbara seemed so far away now.

Okay, one thing at a time—back to my perfect husband. He worked hard every day. I always had a bed to sleep in, food to eat, and nice clothes. Yes, he gave me a home.

I have never known anyone as clean as Frank. He spent more time grooming than I did. He took a bath every night. I watched him clean his nails, clean the inside of his ears, dry between his toes, powder his feet, brush his teeth, and gargle with Listerine every day. He put lotion on his face after shaving. Frank's clothes had to be soft and clean so they would not irritate his skin. Only then would Frank be ready to get in his fresh clean bed. Everything in Frank's world was spotless.

Sunday was the only day Frank didn't work at his job. He washed and waxed his car. He put brown paper sacks on the floor of the car to rest our feet on. He got upset if my feet got on the carpet of his car.

The best thing that could happen would be if we both changed. He could be less particular, and I could be more particular. The problem was I could not talk to Frank. I believed that if I told him the things in my heart, he would not love me. I knew he wanted the perfect person, someone like I had married. If he really knew me, he would not love me. Even my own mother could not love me. I just wanted to go to bed and never get up, just live in my dreams forever.

I could not go back to bed. I needed to wash breakfast dishes, make the bed, and straighten the apartment. I needed to go to the Laundromat, do our clothes, come home and iron the clothes and put them away. I needed to prepare a good dinner for Frank.

I never knew what time Frank would get off work. I always had my bath, makeup, and hair done by 5 PM. Sometimes he didn't get home until 10:00. He was such a hard worker. How could I live like this? I could try one day at a time.

Friday came and I didn't go back to bed after Frank went to work. I did the breakfast dishes, stripped the bed, got dressed, and walked to the Laundromat. I finished the laundry and returned home. I made the bed, put a roast on for dinner, and made a pineapple upside down cake like Frank's mother had taught me. I went out and swept the front porch, came in and put the clothes away, took my bath, and cleaned the bathroom the best it had ever been cleaned. I got dressed and waited for Frank to come home. Neither one of us had turned the TV on. I wasn't sure how to turn it on, and I think Frank was trying to make a point.

Frank came home at 6:00. He seemed a little upset. The first thing he said was that he had stopped and paid off the TV in full. I said, "I thought we had no money." He said he had used our emergency money. He asked if I had prepared for JoAnn and Jackie's visit. I didn't know what to say because I had forgotten about them.

Frank asked me to walk to the back door with him. He asked if I had ever walked out in the backyard. I said no. He asked if I ever looked outside. I said no. The next question was, did I realized we lived in the nicest house on our street? I said no. Frank told me the landlord, who lived upstairs, had rented us the downstairs where his mother lived before we rented it. His sister had taken their mother home with her because she couldn't take care of herself anymore.

I just stood there and looked at him. Frank asked me, "Erma, where will my girls sleep when they get here?"

I said, "I guess with you, and I'll sleep on the couch."

Frank asked, "And that doesn't bother you?"

I said no.

Frank seemed to be getting very upset. He said he didn't know how to get through to me. Nothing seemed to matter to me. He asked if I had ever really looked at his car, and I said, "No, not really." He told me it was one of the nicest cars they made and he cared a lot about it. He said his point was I seemed to care about nothing. He said I walked around in a dream world. He said he bet I hadn't noticed the antique furniture in our apartment. Frank said that if we had smoked or had children, the man would not have rented to us.

I couldn't understand what Frank wanted from me. I couldn't think of anything to say. Was he going to yell at me? He took me by my shoulders and said he wished he could shake me and wake me up. He said I was sweet and would give someone the shirt off my back, but I gave nothing of myself. He said I cared about nothing and wouldn't care if we lost everything.

I wanted to cry, scream, and beat on him until he hurt. I wanted to scream at him that I had lost my mother, my brothers, my sister, all of my family. I had lost Aunt Mary, Billy, and Pap. I had lost my childhood, and he was standing there talking about a stupid car, a backyard, an apartment.

Would these things still be as important to him if he lost his girls and his loving family? I was a shell, but he was worse. He loved a car. I had to stop, stop thinking about it. His eyes were closed; he couldn't see what was important in life. Maybe no one can until they lose it.

I tried to think. *No, there's nothing I could lose at this point in my life that could hurt me, except maybe Frank.* My love for him was like a splinter. It hurt to leave it in, and it would hurt to remove it, but I would heal. I would go on. I would survive. Frank was trying to make something out of nothing.

I needed to get away by myself and think. I wondered if my buying the TV had caused all of this commotion. How do you learn to care about a backyard and a car? I wish I could sleep forever and ever.

We stopped talking. We sat down and ate dinner. Frank didn't say anything else, and I had no answers—nothing, just nothing.

It was Saturday, time to get his daughters. Frank worked until 1:30, came home, took a bath, and we got ready to leave.

JoAnn and Jackie were smart and pretty. They loved their daddy. I could tell this by the way they looked and acted whenever he was around. I also knew Frank adored his girls.

Frank's JoAnn was the caretaker. I could tell this right away. She was more outgoing and had excellent self-esteem. She was a beautiful little girl with sparkling eyes and a loving face. She seemed to love everybody, not just her daddy, and she seemed to take charge even at a young age. I was amazed by her confidence.

Jackie was also a beautiful child. She was quieter than her sister. She was on guard, more cautious. She was not as free with her hugs and kisses. Only with her daddy was she free with her affections; with everyone else she was reserved. When Frank first introduced me to her, I was so afraid she would not let me into her world.

Frank told me to sit down and talk with him for a minute. He said he wanted this to be a special time for JoAnn and Jackie. He wanted them to get to know me, and he wanted them to have a good time during the day. He told me he would leave money for us to go downtown to the movies and to go swimming. Frank said we could even eat out once in a while. I kept saying okay, but in my heart I didn't want any of it to happen. I only wanted to be alone.

Off we went to Granny's to pick up Frank's daughters. They were so excited. We all left Granny's early Sunday morning, and we stopped to have dinner. The girls knew exactly what they wanted. I had a hot ham sandwich, and it was wonderful. I had ordered the same thing Frank had ordered, and it was the best sandwich I had ever eaten.

Frank had to go to work early Monday morning. He and I got up at 5 AM. I prepared his usual breakfast. The girls were still in bed asleep when he left for work. I went back to bed, and then JoAnn and Jackie woke me up at 10:00. They got in bed with me, and we talked and laughed. We got up and ate cereal and toast. They were beautiful, with hair so long they could almost sit on it. JoAnn and Jackie had beautiful clothes and were smart and independent.

JoAnn, Jackie, and I decided to walk the four or five blocks downtown and take our swimming suits. Frank had left us $4 each to spend. We went swimming and got an ice cream on the way home. We played in the backyard with the water hose after we got home. This was the happiest I had ever been in my entire life.

The girls and I had a wonderful summer. It was my happiest. Every day was different. We cooked, went swimming three times a week, watched cartoons, and played Old Maid, jacks, and other games. I never knew how much fun those games could be.

Every day at two in the afternoon, I would stop having fun. I would take a bath, clean the house, and fix Frank's dinner. JoAnn and Jackie usually watched TV then. I was so happy I had gotten the TV.

Frank didn't fuss at me during this time, but he did say things like, "We'll talk about this when JoAnn and Jackie go home." I didn't care. I was alive for the first time in my life and loving every minute of my time with the girls.

Our time with the girls flew by, and before I knew it, we were taking them back to granny's.

On our return trip to Bellefontaine, Frank told me playtime was over and I needed to grow up. He told me I was their stepmother and not their sister. I knew why he was upset. The girls kept telling everyone at Grannies how much fun we had when Frank was at work. JoAnn and Jackie told Granny I was different when Frank was home. I was watching Frank's face when they said that, and I think it hurt his feelings. I went over and sat on his lap and told him I had more fun when he was home. I was telling another lie.

One thing I could not stand was to see Frank hurt. Isn't it strange how love works? I loved Frank and never once doubted he was a good man through and through, but just the tone of his voice or a look could hurt me to my inner being. In Frank's mind, his way was the correct way and my way was the wrong way.

The problem was I always had to do everything my way. I understood Frank had a difficult time explaining his instructions to me. He always wanted me to agree and accept his way of thinking and doing. So I agreed. But no matter what I agreed to, I always ended up doing it my way, not Frank's.

At our home in Bellefontaine, things were different now. I knew my way around my neighborhood and downtown. I could go shopping by myself or just walk downtown and enjoying looking around. I went swimming and to the movies by myself. I was always home by 4:00. I took care of my responsibilities and prepared dinner.

Frank and I were getting along okay. Anything he wanted me to do, I agreed to do. That did not mean I would do it Frank's way. I always had a good reason why I ended up doing it my way. I was learning how to lie and manipulate in my life with Frank. It wasn't like it was the first time I had to perfect those skills. They had been my survival tools throughout my childhood and at the children's home.

I wasn't lonely at that point. I was happy. During the day, I still spent a great deal of time with my make-believe family. As my life became easier and less stressful, I spent less time with them, but I always enjoyed it. I was so loved by that family.

One Friday, two young men knocked on our door. They were Mormon missionaries. They were two of the nicest young men I had ever met. They were wearing suits and looked so nice and clean.

They asked me if I believed in God and if I knew anything about the Mormon religion. I told them I knew there was a God and I talked to my guardian angel. I knew nothing about their church.

The missionaries said they wanted to tell me about the Mormons, the Latter Day Saints. I told them okay but I had to start work at 4:00. They asked where I worked, and I replied, "Here." I told them I began working at 4:00 every day. They seemed confused. They said they had never heard a woman refer to homemaking as going to work.

I guess this did seem strange, but not to me. It was a job that started at 4:00. I hated it. My hands were usually burned from cooking and cut from using the kitchen knives. I didn't like anything about being a housewife, but I did love Frank.

The missionaries talked and talked. They asked me to read from one of their books. I told them I did not have my glasses with me. Just one more lie. I wondered which was worse, my lying to them or their knowing a grown woman couldn't read well.

The missionaries stayed until 4:00. They asked if they could return and meet my husband. I said sure but Sunday was the only day he was home all day. I told them Frank worked six days a week.

They asked if we could have a word of prayer, and I said yes. One of the elders asked if I would offer the prayer. I remember thinking, *what should I do?* I had prayed to myself but never out loud and never in front of other people. I didn't know what to say, but if they wanted me to pray, then I would pray.

I remember bowing my head and saying, "God, thank you for the day and that we have a bed and food to eat, Amen." Now that I look back I realize I should have said, "No, I won't pray," but I wasn't good at telling anyone no, even if I didn't know what I was doing. I always tried to do what was asked of me.

Frank came home, took his bath, and we started eating dinner. I told him two missionaries from the Mormon Church had come by and talked to me about the church. I told him they had read to me from the Bible and the Book of Mormon.

Frank was looking strangely at me. He asked if I had let them come into the house alone with me. I said yes. He told me I should never do that again. I said okay. I remember looking at Frank and thinking, *he really loves me and wants to protect me.* I felt very lucky to have Frank. I wanted with all my heart to make him happy.

Frank seemed the happiest when I sat close to him and did not pull away when he kissed me. I vowed right then I would always kiss him back and never pull away again. I could do this. I kept that vow for the next twenty-eight years of our married life.

Frank was so loving and kind to me. He was also hard and demanding of me. He was hard to please and never passed out compliments. He usually pointed out when I made a mistake or if I was slacking in some area.

I have often thought about our first year of marriage. Frank was the answer to my prayer. He gave me a chance to become a better person. He gave me things I had never had—a home, love, simple kindness, but most of all a feeling of being safe and having a position in life. I was Mrs. Frank Steppe. I needed to learn how to make Frank happy and be proud of me.

The missionaries became a big part of our lives. They came often during the week and every Sunday afternoon. They gave us material and books to read.

They asked Frank to read, and I realized Frank could not read very well. He never refused to read when he was asked. He would mispronounce a word or miss a word when he was reading, and I could tell that made him feel embarrassed. So I started reading everything. I hated for anyone to know how dumb I was, but I would rather they know about me than have Frank feel bad about his reading skills.

The missionaries gave us several weeks of discussions. Finally they came to the Word of Wisdom. We were okay in that area. Neither of us smoked or drank. Frank did have a cup of coffee at breakfast, but he said my coffee was so terrible he wouldn't mind giving coffee up.

We started going to church and I enjoyed it. Frank gave me some money to buy a dress and some dress shoes. I started doing my hair and wearing makeup. I felt very pretty.

The time came when the missionaries asked if we wanted to be baptized. Frank asked me what I thought about this. The whole time the missionaries were teaching us, Frank and I were praying together on our knees every night.

We were reading the Book of Mormon and the Bible together. That night, after we prayed, I told Frank I wanted to be baptized. He said okay but that he wanted to wait awhile to be baptized; in the meantime, he would go to church with me.

I was reading a book by David O. McKay, and in it he said that a man and wife should be baptized together whenever possible. I told Frank I would wait for him until he was ready. I could tell that he really wanted me to be baptized because Frank had decided by the next Sunday that we would be baptized together instead of waiting.

Chapter 17
THE MORMON CHURCH—
A NEW WAY OF LIFE

That started our lives together as Mormons, and I have never regretted that decision. It started a whole new way of life for us as a family. We went to church together every Sunday and prayed together every night. Being a member of the church made me more aware of Frank's role as head of the house and my role as wife and homemaker. It brought peace to my life and made me feel more normal. I began reading and learning on a daily basis.

The company Frank worked for always partied about every three months. I didn't enjoy those outings. I knew I was different from the other women. They always had their hair teased high and wore lots of makeup. I thought they looked like someone you would see on TV. Most of them wore lots of jewelry. I only had my wedding ring, and it bothered me to wear it. I would get my finger wet under the ring and it would itch. I would take the ring off to stop the itching. Frank would ask me where it was and why I wasn't wearing it.

I really didn't like the women or the men. I always felt like the men looked at me like I was an apple ready to be picked. I knew that look and didn't want any part of it. As I watched, I could tell that was why some of the women dressed as they did. I could not understand why any woman would want to put ideas like that in a man's head.

It was at these parties that I realized how different I was. I did not want to be a piece of fruit waiting to be picked. I had already been picked while I was plain and green. When that happens, you never become ripe; you just shrink and disappear, or you rot and die. I have seen many children do both.

I remember one girl at the children's home talking about having sex with her stepfather. She enjoyed it. She would talk about the things he did to her. She said she really loved him and she knew he loved her. Her experiences were nothing like mine. Mom's men didn't care anything about me or whether they hurt me. Most of the time, I never saw them again. Only one man never went away for good. He always returned. Bill came back time after time. I didn't rot or die, but he did destroy something inside of me. That part of me just closed up and had warning bells that went off in my head telling me what to do to protect myself.

One part I do not understand now is why I didn't fight back as a child. I remember the very first time it happened and the feeling of being powerless, worthless, and dirty. Now as an adult, whenever I'm around a forceful, demanding person, I tend to fold up and feel intimidated.

Being a member of the Mormon Church and being married to Frank, I started becoming a more complete person. I started reading recipes and taking more pride in our home and possessions. I was feeling safe, happy, and loved. Joining the church was the best thing Frank and I ever did. I attended a meeting called Relief Society. It taught me more about being a wife and a mother than any college could.

The Mormon Church opened a new way of life for us.. The membership in Bellefontaine was small, and the Mormon Church stressed family and education.

Frank and I spent a long time making our decision to have children. At this point, I really wanted to be a mother. Finally, Frank said he didn't care, so we stopped using birth control. I became pregnant soon after. I had morning sickness from the start. I woke up in the middle of the night vomiting.

I went to the doctor and he told me I was about six weeks pregnant. The doctor prescribed a drug to stop the morning sickness. I didn't take any of the drugs because at that point I was taking everything about the church seriously. I was afraid of even taking an aspirin. That was okay because I never had a headache during my pregnancy. I later learned that the drug the doctor had prescribed for me was very dangerous. It was discovered that this drug, thalidomide, caused all kinds of birth defects. Some children were born with missing limbs.

Frank's company finished the job building the road from Bellefontaine to Columbus. Over the weekend, we went to Columbus and Frank talked to his old boss. Frank told me he would be starting work Monday morning. We had another weekend of moving.

For some reason, all I could do was cry. I think it was because I didn't want to move and leave my friends at church, and I loved my neighbors. I just didn't want to start over again. I was afraid and I didn't want to be lonely.

We moved into a one-bedroom furnished apartment and I hated it. It smelled of cigarette smoke, and the neighbors fought all the time. We went to church on Sunday and it was so big that it had two wards. I was uncomfortable. Everyone was nice, but I just couldn't seem to adjust. It was like returning again to my past. I had no roots and I was pregnant. I resented Frank for taking my friends and security away from me. Frank had no idea I was so unhappy. Moving meant nothing to him. He could make friends with anyone at any time.

One day after we had lived there for about a month, Frank got in an argument with the next-door neighbor. The man was cursing in the hallway. Frank told the man he needed to be inside his apartment if he was going to act like a jerk. We moved again that weekend. I didn't like that place either. I stopped going to church, and I was sleeping night and day. I had no energy.

I was about six months pregnant and had only been to a doctor one time. We had to wait for our insurance to kick in before I could go again. I went to a doctor for the second time when I was eighth months pregnant. He could not believe I had no prenatal care. I was anemic. He said I was sleeping so much because my iron level was low.

Frank came home and told me we were moving to an apartment in the home of his boss. We moved that weekend. Our baby was born three weeks later. Frank drove me to the hospital, and I was in labor for twenty-one hours. I thought I was dying. I wanted to cry and scream, it hurt so badly, but Frank was crying all through my labor. I kept patting his hand and telling him I was okay. I told him not to be upset. Down deep, I wanted him to leave so I could cry and not have to be the strong one.

Frank saw our baby first. I was so excited. Frank came in my room to see me, and I asked him if we had a boy or girl. Frank said we had a baby boy with bright red hair, and he said he didn't like red hair.

I started crying and told him to get out. I told him I hated him. He looked so hurt, but I couldn't understand why Frank didn't think about my feelings. How could he talk about our baby like that? I wished I was dead.

They brought my baby boy to me, and he was so beautiful, so soft and sweet. I gave my heart to him. How could someone love as much as we love our children?

The nurse said she would show me how to nurse my baby. My baby boy was hungry and didn't have any problems nursing. Frank stayed with me while I nursed our son. He held our baby boy, and I could tell Frank loved our son.

I counted all of his fingers and toes. He was so beautiful, so perfect. The nurse came back for my little boy. I did not want them to take him back to the nursery, but she said I had to rest and she would bring him back in four hours.

Our baby came home with us three days later. We named him Charles Bryan Steppe. Frank's father named our son. I had told Pa Steppe if Frank and I had a son, he could name him. Our son was the first grandchild to carry on the Steppe name. We called him Bryan and he was my whole world. Frank was still working six days a week.

Bryan would go to bed in his bassinet, but when he woke to nurse, I would put him in bed with us. Bryan started waking earlier for his feeding. Soon he was sleeping only an hour and then he would wake up and I would put him in our bed with us. Finally we just put him in our bed, and the three of us slept like babies. I was comfortable sleeping close to my baby.

We started going to church every Sunday when Bryan was one week old. At home, Bryan and I would play all day long. We played patty cake and peek-a-boo, and I read lots of stories to him.

Frank and I argued most Sundays. I got upset whenever he scolded Bryan or wanted to take him out in the hallway at church for making noise. One Sunday after church, I shouted at Frank after we got in the car. I told him I would never go back to church and he would come home one day and we would be gone. I knew this was the only power I had over Frank. He did love both Bryan and me. From then on, Frank calmed down in church and Bryan didn't have to act like a grownup during services.

Now I was staying home every day. I had to take a bus when I went to the store. I did not drive. The only place I went to was church. I don't know how we managed. We never bought clothes, and I don't remember shopping, except for groceries.

Frank loved us and took good care of us. He was a doting father. Every night, he would get in the tub and I would hand him Bryan and they would bathe together. Bryan loved bath time with his father.

We got up every morning at 5:30. I would nurse Bryan while Frank ate his breakfast, and then Frank would play with Bryan while I packed Frank's lunch. Frank would go to work, and Bryan and I would go back to bed until 9 or 10 AM.

I started having morning sickness again, and this time I knew I was pregnant. The company Frank worked for had decided to cancel the insurance on their employees. Frank said I was healthy, so I did not go to the doctor since we had no insurance.

Frank decided I would go to his parents' house because a nearby hospital there charged only a $100 for a doctor to deliver a baby and I could have a one-night stay at that hospital.

I wanted to sleep all the time. I had no strength or energy. I started spotting. A German lady who lived upstairs told me that this happens sometimes. She was wonderful and she was my friend. She told me to stay off my feet as much as possible. She would come downstairs and get Bryan and keep him with her all day while I rested on the couch. I could tell that Bryan loved her.

I still fixed Frank's breakfast and lunch, and I still got up at 4 PM and took care of my responsibilities. I did not want Frank to know I was spotting. I don't know why that was important to me. Maybe it was because I didn't want him to send me to his mother's. The spotting didn't last long, and I will always be grateful to my upstairs friend for her kindness.

Frank and I tried to count back to my last period to figure out when I would need to go to his mother's. The last weekend in May, Bryan and I went to Granny's house, and Frank's dad took me to the doctor. I was low on iron. The doctor was concerned and wanted me to take iron and vitamins.

Our counting was off quite a bit. I ended up staying at Granny's until July 30th. That was when our only daughter, Constance Rae Steppe, was born.

I awoke with serious labor pains and told Granny it was time I went to the hospital. Granny got Pa from the barn. Pa said he would need a plastic sheet for his truck seat in case my water broke in the truck. He didn't want a mess. Granny and Pa worked on the plastic sheet idea for some time. I was in terrible pain. I told them we really needed to get going, so Pa and I started for the hospital.

My pains were getting harder and closer together. Pa drove about 30 mph, and I was sure I was going to have the baby in the truck. I kept telling Pa to go faster. My pains were coming fast and hard. He continued at 30 mph, and I was getting scared. Pa pulled off the road and let a school bus pass us. I shouted at him to go faster. He never went over 30 mph, and now we had a school bus in front of us stopping to pick up schoolchildren. The pain was almost unbearable.

We made it to the hospital, and Pa parked all the way out in the middle of the parking lot so no one would hit or scratch his truck. I told him I could not walk, so Pa started the truck and drove me to the front door. I was taken inside in a wheelchair.

I was alone in my room and was in horrible pain. I wanted something for the pain. They had given me something for pain when I had Bryan, but I was told this hospital did not believe in pain medication. No one had told me anything about this policy. I was screaming at the top of my lungs. I told them they had better give me something for pain or I would tell my husband.

I gave birth to my most precious daughter, and afterward they put me in a big room with several other women. The woman in the bed beside me asked if I had heard that woman screaming and carrying on something awful. I nodded my head yes. The woman said she had given birth to ten children and she had never acted like that or made such horrible noises. She said that woman behaved awfully. I fully agreed with her. I never told her that horrible woman screaming was me.

While I was gone, Frank had found us another place to live. The apartment we had was too small for four people.

I gave birth to my baby girl on Friday. Frank worked a half day on Saturday and then came to Granny's. On Sunday morning, we all loaded up and went back to Columbus.

I was weak and dizzy and everything on me hurt. Connie cried a lot. Frank was tired and irritable. It was a horrible trip home.

When we arrived home, I was so weak I couldn't do anything. I had no breast milk for Connie. I guess not having anything to eat or drink all the way home had affected my breast milk. We had a can of Carnation Milk, so I put it in a bottle and gave it to Connie. She had a problem with the hard nipple but she drank.

The next morning, I had my milk supply again, but I sure felt bad. I had some vitamins and iron pills left, so I started taking them. I began feeling better after a few days.

Bryan was a handful. He was a high-strung, busy little boy. Bryan was fourteen months old when Connie was born. I was alone with my children, and it felt good not to have other people around me all the time.

Being a new mother of two babies was a lot to deal with daily. When Connie turned six weeks old, I had to find a doctor for her six-week check up. I found one on the corner of Main Street and Como; we lived on Como. I got Bryan and Connie ready, and we walked to the doctor's office. Connie was in a baby stroller, and Bryan was in front of me with his hands on the stroller and my hands over his.

The doctor checked me first while the nurse watched my children. He said I was fine and healing nicely. Then he checked Connie, and she was beautiful and healthy. I was proud of my beautiful little girl. Everything about Connie was perfect. No one could have asked for a better baby. Bryan was such a good little boy all during our doctor's visit. Everyone thought he was so cute.

In our home, we had one twin bed. This was our first unfurnished apartment. It was a duplex with three bedrooms upstairs and a bath. Downstairs we had a living room, a kitchen, and a dining room. We had a basement with a washer and dryer, the first items we bought.

We started buying furniture for our home, but we only bought one piece at a time because we always paid in full with cash. We had a table with four chairs in the kitchen, and I put two chairs in the living room so we could sit and watch TV.

We lived in this duplex for two years, and then Frank got transferred to Dayton, Ohio, and we moved again. We lived in Dayton for two years and then moved back to Columbus. I had to get a driver's license. I had studied the learner's manual for over one year and passed the test when I took it.

Frank's daughters came to Columbus to spend the summer with us. At the end of the summer, Jackie went back to Booneville and JoAnn stayed with us and went to school. Frank and I spent many hours talking about JoAnn. She had been working at a restaurant and had to quit to start school. There was no way Frank was going to let JoAnn live the same lifestyle she had lived in Booneville. She was used to the best.

Frank was working long hours and had a church calling as a ward missionary. It was his responsibility to visit part-member families in our ward, and he had a companion to go with him. Part-member families were those in which only the husband or wife was a Mormon.

Frank and JoAnn were at each other constantly. He did not like the way she dressed or the way she wore her makeup. JoAnn had hemmed one of Connie's little dresses, and Frank was furious with her about it. He said it was too short for Connie and he made JoAnn take out the hem right then.

I started working part time at the same restaurant JoAnn had worked. I wasn't sure I liked Frank at this time in our marriage. He was working six days a week, doing missionary work three nights a week, and going to church on Sunday. Frank was on edge, tired, and irritable.

Frank fell at work and hurt his lower back. He had picked up an old ladder, climbed up it, and one of the rungs broke. Frank fell and landed with his lower back across a 2 x 4. He went to the doctor, and the doctor put him in a removable wraparound brace. Frank was supposed to wear it on the job. The doctor wanted him to stay off work for a couple of weeks, but Frank went to work anyway.

Frank's nerves were wearing thin, and it showed in our family and in his dealings with our neighbors. We shared a clothesline with our neighbors. They had a big dog and tied the dog to the clothesline. Frank complained to the neighbors about the noise, and things got bad. Frank stepped in dog poop. Someone poisoned the dog, and then things really got worse.

My feelings at this time were all mixed up. I sure did hate my life. It was like Frank and JoAnn were in charge of everything. My home was not my own; JoAnn had so much more self-confidence than I had. She was mature and knew what she wanted. At the same time, I also enjoyed having JoAnn live with us. I did love her deeply, but she and Frank together was like being in a war zone. They were oil and water; they couldn't agree on anything.

I was spending my tip money on clothes for Bryan and Connie to wear to church. Frank and I disagreed over this. He felt it was wasteful, but I was determined our children would have nice clothes.

JoAnn decided to go home one weekend, and Frank said I had to go with them to take JoAnn home. I said no. I had decided I didn't want to live with Frank anymore. I wanted him to move out and leave us. Frank said he wasn't going anywhere. He came to my job and wanted me to go to Booneville with him and the children. I refused. All I wanted to do was to go home after work, be alone, and have some time to think. He left the restaurant, and I returned to work.

Frank drove back to the restaurant and asked me again to go with them to Booneville. I went outside to tell JoAnn good-bye and to kiss Bryan and Connie. Frank told me if I didn't go with them then I would have no right to see our children.

This was a terrible time for all of us. I felt I was wrong to go against his will, but I really hated Frank at this time and my reasons were many.

Frank was also the only person in the world I completely trusted. To me, he was the only person I could ever live with and be happy. I couldn't seem to get my feelings straight or my reasons. I just knew I couldn't live like this any longer.

Frank blamed me for everything. Things that were small to me were a big deal to Frank. Something like the children's wagon being left down the driveway was a major deal. Frank would shout at me. Why didn't I make the children put their things away before they came in for the night? Frank had a temper and showed it often.

I did not go to Booneville with Frank and the children. After I finished working, I went home to be by myself and think.

Frank was killing himself working six days a week and doing missionary work three nights a week. On those three nights, he would rush home, bathe, eat, and join his companion who was usually waiting for him. They would then visit with part-family members. We would spend all day Sunday at church.

I was not happy and did not like the fast pace of our lives. JoAnn had wanted to go back to Booneville, and I didn't blame her. She wasn't the problem. It was just everything mixed together. Frank wasn't happy, and I knew part of his unhappiness was my fault. I couldn't seem to do it all—everything that Frank wanted.

Bryan started first grade and he needed school clothes. Considering Frank's reaction when I bought the children church clothes, I knew he would not see how important this was to me. I could not sneak enough money to buy Bryan school clothes.

JoAnn's going home would solve some of our problems. She had all the wants and needs of a normal teenager, and Frank sure did not understand any of that.

These two little girls would become a big part of my life. We had wonderful times sharing secrets, watching TV, swimming, cooking, eating, and having tickle time. These are very special memories I will always cherish. We were friends and grew into adulthood together. There has never been any doubt about my love for these two little girls, my friends.

I felt Frank and I needed to go somewhere and make a fresh start. I waited for Frank to come home, and we talked about my idea. Frank felt the same way. We discussed what our options were. I could not work with two small children, and we had no health care. Frank could not pay all the bills without me working. We decided to move to Booneville. Frank would work in Columbus until he found work in Kentucky. We moved to Booneville the next month.

A friend of Frank's had an apartment over a store in Booneville. We moved into this apartment. The man's wife was a wonderful person, and she and I became good friends.

Bryan started school in Booneville. Frank would come home on Friday nights and leave on Sundays. During the week, the only place we went was a matinee at a little theatre. I got to know the old lady that ran the place. She would let us go in free once a week.

We only lived in Booneville for three months.

Chapter 18
BUCKHORN AND REVIVING THE PAST

Buckhorn was hiring house parents for the Buckhorn Children's Center. Frank and I went for an interview to be substitute house parents. Frank had never done this kind of work, and I had never told him that I had lived it most of my life. By working as house parents, we would live in the same home with a house parent's apartment, but serve as parent roles to the children living there. This included Frank supervising work camps, routine maintenance, and all grounds work. He thought he would like working at Buckhorn since all our living expenses, even the food, were included. Frank's goal was to put our entire salary in the bank, which we did for four years.

We got the job. The Buckhorn Children's Center had three dorms—one for girls of all ages, one for the small boys, and one for the older boys. Frank and I would work with all three groups as substitute house parents. Each month, the regular house parents would get a week off while we worked in their place. Each dorm had house parent's apartments, and for three weeks we moved from one dorm to another. Our family had one week off per month. That was every house parent's schedule. I remember thinking, *this is just like being in the children's home.* I was twenty-four years old when we began our job at Buckhorn.

The first year, I didn't go to town or anywhere without Frank. The people at Buckhorn were very nice. They had a store on campus, and we shopped there most of the time. During that time, our children had nice clothes and seemed to enjoy their lives.

Looking back now, I feel like I was living in a fog. It felt like I had stepped back in time. I hated working with the older boys. They reminded me of the boys where I went to school, the boys that always made fun of me. I didn't like the big boys' cottage. It seemed spooky to me.

I really enjoyed staying with the small boys. We would watch cartoons, play games, and pop popcorn. We all seemed to enjoy our one week off. Frank and our family would go to Granny and Pa Steppe's and visit with Frank's sisters.

I was having a difficult time because I was never alone. I've always seemed to need my alone time to pull myself together. Everyone seemed to believe we were living a slow-paced life, but I did not feel that way. I felt on edge all the time.

I had to wake the children, mine included, and make sure they all got out of bed. I had to supervise them getting dressed and help to get breakfast for between ten and twelve people every morning. The children had to make their beds, do dishes, and be ready for school at 8 AM. On Saturday, we all cleaned the cottage. On Sundays, we went to church. Connie and Bryan were both in school.

I became pregnant with Keith Allen while we were working at Buckhorn. Frank seemed happy about the news. We were looking forward to having a little baby again.

Connie had made friends with our neighbor's children. They were the house parents for the girl's cottage. Bryan was playing with a little boy whose parents worked at another cottage.

Frank loved working with the other employees during the day, but I was so lonely. It seemed like I had no one. It wasn't anyone's fault but my own. To have a close friend, you have to open up and share information. I couldn't do that with anyone. All my life, when talking with people, I just had the here and now. My past, my before Frank, was gone. I lived in constant fear that someone would find out I was no one. I remember thinking, *what would they say if they knew I was just like these children?* I'm working with these children and trying to help them—but inside I'm just like them.

Frank saw everything cut and dried. You did the right thing. You worked hard and said what you thought. I was guarded in all areas. I was always thinking, *don't say too much, and don't let them know you're not as good as they are. Hide your feelings. Hide who you really are, and keep hidden all your secrets.*

Don't talk too much and don't let everyone know you're so damaged. Maybe that's why counseling is so important. It helps people to open up and get past these kinds of problems.

We had staff meetings every Monday morning. I remember walking down the hill to those meetings and thinking, *I hope Frank doesn't hurt someone's feelings in our meeting today.* He usually did. Frank was very critical of how everyone else did their job. He complained about everything. Some cottages were not clean enough, some cottages had garbage in their yard, some cottages didn't watch their children closely enough, some cottages didn't keep their children quiet, some cottages didn't make the children dress correctly, and so on. Frank complained about everything and everyone.

Everyone was offended at one time or another by Frank. He didn't understand social workers, and he really didn't understand children. Frank believed children should do as they were told and keep quiet.

The director came to our cottage to ask me to please be at the staff meetings when Frank was in attendance. The director felt I was able to keep Frank from getting in trouble when he stated his opinions. What the director didn't know was that it took everything I had in me to ask Frank to stop talking or to quit putting his foot in his mouth. Frank still usually continued with his opinions anyway.

It was a good thing Buckhorn was in Eastern Kentucky. It seemed like most of the men and some of the women agreed with some of Frank's philosophy. Other workers, who came from out of state, especially from the north, had a difficult time agreeing with the philosophy of the Buckhorn staff. Our staff meetings very often got hot and loud. Then there was me—I was the peacemaker. I tried to smooth everything out and keep the peace. I tried to point out the good on both sides.

The house parents for the girls' cottage quit, and Frank and I took over their position. Our lives became a little easier, at least for me. We didn't have to move around so much.

I gave birth to Keith Allen on January 21st. He was a perfect baby. He was so wonderful, and all I wanted to do was hold him. Frank told me to quit kissing his head so much while we were in staff meetings. That hurt my feelings. I loved my baby so much, and Connie and Bryan seemed to enjoy having a baby brother. All the girls wanted to hold him. My little boy was never alone.

That fall, I decided to go back to school. I knew I needed to get my G.E.D. to be able to enroll in college. I needed for my children to see that Frank and I could learn to read without stumbling over the words. I wasn't sure what grade I had finished. I think maybe it was the eighth grade.

I wrote to Barbara and told her I was having a problem getting my school records. I told her I thought the problem was that I had so many last names—at least five. I had used Bill's last name until the state took custody of me. When they told Bill he would be paying child support on his children, he let them know I was not his child. Every time I went to a foster home, I assumed their last name. I never know my last name until I had to produce my birth certificate to get married. I told Barbara I wanted to go to Lees Junior College. I asked her if she would write a letter and explain the last name problem to the school counselor there. I gave Barbara his name and address, and once again Barbara took care of all of my problems.

The counselor said everything was fine and I could start as a freshman in the fall. I remember asking him if I had to get my G.E.D., and he said no. He said my grades were great. I wasn't sure what happened, but I was happy to start as a college student. I didn't see my transcripts until I started college at Morehead State University. The school in Meigs County had mailed someone else's transcript to my counselor. She had the same last name as my foster parents. That person had graduated as an honor roll student. That's why I didn't have to get my G.E.D.

Bryan and Connie were in school, and Keith was about eight months old. I only took one class, freshman English, a three-hour course every Monday and Wednesday and every other Friday.

I didn't know anything about English, so I had a hard time with this class. I didn't attend the next semester because the roads were so bad in the wintertime. Sometimes my cottage girls would not have school because of the bad weather. I did take a class the following semester though. The children had summer school with work camps that came from the north for the summer. During this time, I got the same elderly lady to sit with Keith for half a day while I attended classes. She was great with Keith, and he seemed to love her. Bryan and Connie were in summer school with the other children.

We had been at Buckhorn for a few years. A girl in our cottage had a serious acting out problem. She seemed delinquent and older than the other girls. One night, she and three other girls ran away. Frank and the other staff went looking for them. They found the girls at the older boys' cottage, and Frank was furious. He gave all of them castor oil. He told them if they wanted to run, then he would help them run. The girls were up and down all night going to the bathroom, and they complained of their stomachs hurting.

The next night at bedtime, the sixteen-year-old got upset. Frank told her to get in bed. She said no. Frank put her in the bed, forcefully. The next day, our director paid me another visit. He told me that Frank and I would probably need to find another job. It was possible that Frank could have charges filed against him. The social worker was away for the month, and he was afraid that when she returned we could have a serious problem. I told him I would talk to Frank, but I knew Frank would not see anything wrong with what he had done. I also knew he could be in serious trouble.

I had lived at the children's home. I knew Mr. G. could only hit someone on the bottom. That was the law. It had been in Our Rights hanging on the wall. The rules were: paddling only on the behind, no smacking on the face or bumping heads.

I asked Frank to sit and talk with me after everyone was in bed. We sat in our living room, and I told Frank that because of the incident with the sixteen-year-old, we could get in serious trouble. Frank could not understand why. He said she got exactly what she deserved. I explained to Frank that the social worker would return from Vermont in less than a month and she could and probably would file charges against Frank. She was that kind of social worker.

We decided it would be best if we moved. I would stay at Buckhorn until Frank had a job and a place for us to live. Our week off was coming up, so we decided to go to Bath County. The job Frank wanted was in Mt. Sterling at the Hobart's Plant. We told everyone at Buckhorn that since we had three children we needed to get our family together and have a real home life. We also used the excuse that I wanted to go to Morehead State.

I knew down deep that I could never carry a full class load at the university. I could hardly read, write, or spell. When I took my driver's test, I had to study the manual for more than a year first.

Frank started working at Hobart's shortly after he applied for the job, and I stayed at Buckhorn until they found new house parents for the girls' cottage. We moved in one weekend. Frank had to be at work Monday morning.

Chapter 19
BATH COUNTY—FAMILY LIFE

Bryan and Connie started school at Salt Lick Elementary. We lived in a big two-story house on Route 60 in Bath County. I didn't go to college the first semester. We needed to settle in our new home and positions. We started going to church every Sunday and became very active members.

Ever since Frank had fallen off the ladder and hurt his back in Columbus, his back had often caused him a lot of pain. Frank had a short fuse with his family, and our good times were few and far between. He wanted us home when he was home. Frank didn't want to know about any problems when he was home, and that was fine with me. I've always loved Frank, but I wasn't happy with him and sometimes I didn't like him. I was never a good disciplinarian. I believe this caused some of the problems my children have now. We all just did our thing when Frank wasn't home.

We all played the part of a good little family when Frank was home. I became an expert at manipulating and lying. We were a dysfunctional family. We didn't fight, smoke, or drink. We went to church every Sunday, but we were not a happy family and our home was not a happy one.

I lived only a few hours from where my mother had settled down with a man named Albert. She had married and seemed to be getting her life together.

During this time, my children and I went to visit her once a year.

The years just seemed to roll by. Bryan moved to Beattyville and got married, and Connie got engaged. I had checked out my money market savings to pay for her wedding. Connie was working and going to beauty school.

Frank and I were having problems. I went to Ohio and brought Mom home with me so she could be a part of her granddaughter's wedding festivities. I believed this was a good thing.

Mom seemed to enjoy that week very much. She made only one comment that indicated that she really hadn't changed. Mom said, "How could you spend money like that on her wedding when your mom is so poor?" I didn't answer her. I took Mom home a few days after Connie's wedding.

Connie and her husband, Doug, needed some furniture, and Frank and I needed some new items, so I gave Connie some of our old pieces of furniture. Connie and I went shopping for living room furniture and kitchen items for my house. I made the payments with my paycheck. During this time, I was working two jobs. One job was a state job and the other job was at our local hospital. I used one of my work checks to pay for the furniture. Frank was furious about this and refused to talk to me for a long time. This was only a symptom of the problems in our marriage.

Doing for your children is something a parent does to make their child's life just a little bit easier. Frank never believed this. No one could love their children more than Frank, but he just didn't believe in spending or using money. He believed once our children had gone from our home, they were on their own.

Frank has a strong personality, but no one could say he wasn't good, honest, and kind. I do have a hard time giving of myself, but I would give anything I had to my children.

We weren't the Brady Bunch or the Cleaver family, but I have always thought of my children as being very independent and strong. They are very set in their ways and bounce back from hard times. When a door closes, they find another door to open.

When you start weighing what makes a successful person, I'm sure my faults and shortcomings are many. I also know that my children were dressed as well and maybe better than most of the other children in their school. They were popular at school and had a good spot in the community. They could always be proud of their home.

Our homes were not the best, but they were houses we could all be proud of. They could match any child in their class with their social skills.

One day, Mom called me and told me her husband had died. She said she had no transportation and her house was falling in around her. She was renting a two-bedroom house that was owned by a rock quarry in Meigs County. She paid only $10 a month in rent. I'm sure if she hadn't been living there they would have torn the house down long ago.

I took off work the next two days and went to see her. I couldn't stand the thought of her living in such conditions and having no food. I had been sending her a little money every week without Frank's knowledge.

I arrived to find that someone had taken her to the store and had given her a load of wood. It rained while I was there, and her roof leaked in several places. Her fireplace had fallen, so her source of heating was gone. She said she wanted to move to Kentucky, so I brought her home with me.

I began looking for a little place for her to rent. Renting was expensive, and Mom's income was only $420 a month. I discovered that she couldn't afford to rent and she couldn't afford to buy because she had no credit and her income was too low.

I finally found a little two-bedroom house that was only a couple of miles from my house. She would be near me, and I could take care of her. The house cost $18,000 and the monthly payment would be $250. I bought the house and did not tell Frank about this new financial adventure of mine.

I moved Mom in the next week. We had a hard time getting her furniture, but finally we got everything she needed and her little house looked great. The furniture had been a financial drain on me, but Mom seemed so happy. About a month later, she told me she needed to go back to Pomeroy for a couple of weeks. I took her to Pomeroy, and Mom said she would stay with Aunt Mary while she was there.

On the appointed date I was getting ready to go to Meigs County to pick Mom up at Aunt Mary's, Mom called me and told me she was already back at her house and she wanted me to come right away. I drove the few miles and arrived to find that all the furniture I had gotten her was sitting in the yard with a Yard Sale sign. An eighty-six-year-old man was sitting in Mom's kitchen.

Mom told me she had gotten married and they were going to use his furniture, so she was selling her furniture. She and the man had already moved in all of his furniture. She told me he had a truck and was able to drive her wherever she needed to go, so I just left. I should have known. As usual, Mom had her own plans and they did not include me.

I didn't go back. I had learned at a very young age that when Mom was involved with a man I needed to stay away. I did continue to make the house payments and pay the insurance on the house.

Mom called me a few weeks later. She wanted me to come right away. Her new man had loaded his pickup truck with his furniture, hired a helper, and moved back to Ohio, leaving her in an empty house. He was gone, and she didn't have a box to sit on. Once again, I searched for furniture for her home. She had nothing and needed everything. So for the second time, I furnished her house. Of course, Frank knew nothing about any of this.

Twice I had furnished Mom's home, but it would not be the last time. Mom always sold her furniture in a yard sale whenever her husband returned with his furniture. All this furniture was a serious drain on my finances, and Frank did not know.

Mom's new husband was old and lonely. He really only wanted someone to care about him and take care of him. Mom stated several times, "He was a good catch."

Knowing Mom, I think she thought he would die. She hoped he would leave her with some money. Finally, he sold his house and moved in with Mom permanently. He had a little money, so he put a new roof on Mom's little house. He also had a big porch built so they could sit outside. When he died four years later, he had no money to leave her.

Mom had lied to her new husband and told him that she owned the little house. That was why he had added the porch and put on a new roof. Like everyone else, he believed Mom's lies. Her new husband wanted his name on the deed to Mom's house. He felt this was only fair since he had made the improvements.

I had given Mom my phone number at work—big mistake! Mom wanted something. She told me she paid the electric bill, mowed the yard, and paid the gas bill. She said she had a lot of money tied up in that house.

I took Mom to the store one day after that, and she started going on about the house. She told me she wanted the house and she wanted the deed in her name. She wanted me to give her the house. She went on and on, raging. When we got back to her house, she didn't even say good-bye.

I arrived at work and the phone rang. I picked it up. Mom said, "You need to fire Erma Steppe. She's no good!" and she slammed the phone down. Mom must have thought I was the secretary.

A couple of days later, I got a personal loan. I only owed $4,000 on the house. I met with Mom and her new husband at a lawyer's office, and I gave Mom the house. All I wanted to do was get away from her.

At this time, Frank and I were at odds. Bryan, Connie, and JoAnn were married. Jackie lived independently in Florida. Keith was our only child at home. One night, Keith came home late with his ear pierced. Frank grabbed the earring out of Keith's ear and stomped it. I was furious with Frank. We did not talk for days. Our marriage needed to come to an end.

I still loved Frank. He had so much goodness inside of him, but Frank had no tolerance for the faults of others. Frank had been my protector. He had loved me and taken care of me through twenty-eight years of my faults and ignorance. I had three beautiful, healthy, intelligent children with Frank. Our children were filled with goodness because of Frank. I was Mrs. Frank Steppe for twenty-eight years.

I have never been sorry that Frank was the father of my children. He was an honest, hardworking man who loved his children and me. I knew Frank wasn't perfect, but he sure came close.

I had always thought of myself as being damaged and abnormal. I had always thought that I was just a little out of touch with reality. I had a make-believe family, a family I spent hours sitting and daydreaming about.

Now as I look back, I wonder how often I walked around in a fog, not really seeing. I wasn't growing.

I will never be a scholar. I can't seem to read, write, or spell well. I have some trouble remembering things. At college, I was tested and they discovered some disabilities with all kinds of names.

I knew right from wrong. I try to do my best in everything I do. An example of this is all the words I've had to look up in the dictionary while writing this, not to mention the rewrites.

I had another break with my mother. Once again, she was happy without me in her life. She let me know once more that I was no one important to her. She had her new man, and that was all she needed. I did not matter; I was no one.

Mom called me and told me to come to her house right away; she needed to talk to me. I always went to Mom's on Saturday to take her to the store. Her husband could drive and had a truck, but at eighty-six years old, he didn't feel comfortable driving in Morehead.

When I got to Mom's, she met me outside. She told me she wanted me to start a life away from her. She said she was afraid of what I would say, and her new husband didn't know anything about her past. She told me she didn't need me there to mess up her life. This man wasn't like the others. She was sure he had some money.

Mom made it clear she didn't want any of her past to come near him, especially me. I remember standing there and thinking, *my marriage is coming to an end, and now my mother is gone too.* My mom was kicking me out again. If something happened to my mom, this man would get the house—the house I gave up so much for. The house I thought she would love—and then maybe love me for the first time. As she was walking away from me, I remember thinking, *how can she just walk away like I no longer exist? What a strange uncaring woman.* I was nothing to her at that moment.

I watched my mother walk back into her house. I hadn't said a word. I never did when she talked to me like that. I became that little girl, the one she couldn't stand and blamed everything on. I could feel my heart break again. How could a mother tell her child good-bye, walk away, and never look back? Again I thought about how much easier it is to deal with a broken body. The physical pain isn't what destroys a person. It's the terrible hurt inside, the hurt you would give anything to make go away.

Chapter 20
Divorce—Who Knew

I decided I was going to terminate my marriage with Frank. I was living lies. Frank would tell me not to keep anything from him; he wanted to know everything. But on his arrival home, Frank would say he did not want to hear about any problems. His nerves just could not stand anything else. So, I told Frank nothing. We were the perfect family. We had no problems. I handled everything. During our children's growing years, when they had a problem, I took care of it.

I went to the schools. I bought the books and other supplies. I bought the school pictures, jackets, and class rings. I handled our money and paid our living expenses. Frank never set money aside for a family outing. Things like Christmas, a birthday, or a school event, I had to manage myself. I used our money, my money, any money so that we could do normal recreational activities and the children would feel accepted at school and church.

I'm not saying Frank was wrong in his money dealings. I'm saying I did not handle the money the way Frank wanted me to use it. I just wanted our family to have the regular everyday luxuries. I did stay in a financial hole a lot because of my spending.

Everyone seems to think that there has to be some big reason for a couple to get a divorce. They think the couple has fallen out of love. Maybe they have found someone new. Maybe there's a hidden sickness. None of these were true for us. I always loved Frank, and I truly believe Frank loved me. No, there was never another person. If I were going to fall for another person, it would have happened a long time ago when I weighed 125 pounds and was in my twenties, or maybe when I was going to college or enjoying the children's ballgames. No, there was never, ever anyone else.

At one point in our marriage, probably in my thirties, I did go through a flirtatious period. I would mildly flirt with and talk to men at public events. I enjoyed them looking at me and talking to me. My flirting never led to anything else. I wanted no part of a sexual affair. I think that I just wanted someone to see me and think I was pretty and say nice things to me. The sexual part of me had been stolen in my childhood, and I don't believe I ever regained it.

Frank was gone from home most of the week on his job. An affair would have been an easy thing for me to manipulate if I had chosen to do so. I never did.

At this point in my life, I was a middle-aged, overweight woman who only went to church on occasion. I had a strong feeling that I did not want to go to church anymore. I was living a lie. I wanted to leave Frank. I never again wanted to hear him say, "Erma, you need to change ..."

One Saturday night, Frank and I were lying in our bed when he said to me, "I never thought I would be married to a fat woman." I started crying and could not stop. He kept trying to pull me close to him, but I kept pulling away. It was at that time that I made my mind up to leave Frank. After many years, we started accepting that our marriage was failing. Nobody ever does everything right, but Frank came close. We both made mistakes and made bad decisions in our marriage. I accept some of the responsibility for the failure of my marriage.

I went from a dysfunctional child to a dysfunctional adult. I often wonder why one of the greatest tools we have is looking back and seeing all of our mistakes. It's too late to change our mistakes at that point. In life, you don't get a redo.

This time, I would not run away. I would not do that to Frank. I would plan my departure. I would make sure Frank would be okay when I was gone. I knew Frank better than he knew himself. Frank was good looking, neat, clean, and very presentable. He would not stay alone for very long. I knew he would start looking for someone soon after I left. I did not believe he would marry right away because it would take a certain type of woman to suit him.

I had been working at a residential facility for emotionally disturbed children in Lexington, about 45 miles from home, during this time. The job I had came with a cottage I could live in. I knew it would be very hard for me to come up with enough money to pay rent with my income, but living poor was better than I was living now.

I worked in Lexington and drove to Bath County every day at 8 AM and stayed until 3 PM. I went to work from 4:15 until 8 AM the next day. I worked with eight, nine-, and ten-year-old boys. Mom's husband had been involved in a serious accident in his truck, and his driver's license was revoked. She called me, once again, for reconciliation. Once again, I responded to her needs in my off-hours. I knew that leaving Frank would be one of the hardest things I had ever done. I have a fear of causing pain to others, and I knew this would hurt my loved ones. I also knew I had to do it for myself. I would have to be locked away if I did not do it.

The problems that Frank and I had started at our very beginning. Had I been stronger, I would have set limits on Frank, but we came together at the most fragile time in my life. I no longer had Barbara and the children's home as my safety net. My mother had put me out on the streets of Columbus. I had nowhere else to go but with Frank. So Frank ruled our lives, and I had all these problems that were destroying me.

Finally the week came when I called Frank and told him I was not coming home. I told him I needed time to think. This all happened on a Friday night. I sat and cried alone in my cottage all night. Frank called the next day, and I told him I wasn't coming home. His heart was broken, but so was mine. I had to do it. Frank told me we needed to talk in person, but he couldn't take off work. We talked several times the next week.

Frank now had a different slant on our breakup. He was now saying if I wanted to come back, I needed to change some things. He said we would start over. Frank said I needed to let him handle everything dealing with our money. I would need to quit work. Frank said he would arrange for me to meet with the head of our church. Everything he said only made me more determined not to return to Frank.

I have lived sixty-five years. The first seventeen years, I lived in all kinds of conditions and suffered all kinds of abuse, but the thing I couldn't seem to get over was the fact that my mother didn't love me and didn't want me to be part of her life. In fact, she blamed me for all of her faults and problems.

The next twenty-eight years I spent trying to overcome the scars of my childhood. I tried to hide all of my experiences. These experiences made me feel dirty and inadequate. I spent those years trying to be what I thought made a good person. I had to learn how to be a person, an adult, a wife, and a mother. Thanks to Frank and the Mormon Church, I accomplished to some degree most of the things that make someone a productive member in society.

I tried to give my children what I didn't have as a child. To this day, my children and grandchildren are my world. I would swim any river for them—and I don't swim. I know I would have the determination to make it to them.

When I think of Frank, I feel nothing but love. He didn't have a lot to work with. He tried so hard to make me the person, wife, and mother he wanted. He never asked or seemed to care who I was or what happened to me. He was just working to help me develop into the person of his dreams, but I had so far to go. I just couldn't make it, and in the end, I didn't want to. I just wanted to be myself. Dysfunctional as I was, I just wanted peace.

I cleared about $600 a month working at a re-education program. I remember thinking I needed a part-time job. At this time, I was wondering if Frank and I would get back together. I was talking to him on the phone almost every day.

It was Saturday, and Frank called. He said, "If you aren't coming home, I'm getting a divorce." I told him I was so confused and mixed up, I didn't know what I was going to do.

He told me he thought I was trying to get all he had worked so hard for and I wasn't going to get any of what was his. Frank really didn't know me. I would never take the things he had worked for. Things weren't important to me.

I had to take all these pieces and glue them back together so I could function as a person again. I knew I could take care of myself. I ended it with, if he felt he needed to file for a divorce, then do it. A few days later, I got papers and a phone call from Frank's lawyer. He wanted me to meet with Frank and him next week. I said okay.

I remember walking into the attorney's office. I was so nervous. The three of us sat down and I remember thinking, *Frank will know what's best.*

He always had a head for business. His lawyer asked if I had a lawyer, and I said no.

Frank's lawyer had a list of everything we owned. One by one, we went over the list.

1. *Our house, paid in full, value $67,000* — Frank wanted it. I said okay.
2. *Property lot, paid in full* — Frank wanted it. I said okay.
3. *All furniture, paid in full* — Frank wanted it. I said okay.
4. *Boat, paid in full* — Frank wanted it. I said okay.
5. *$3,000 IRA* — Frank wanted it. I said okay. I had spent my $3,000 IRA on Connie's wedding.
6. *Rental property, we owed what it was worth* — Frank wanted it. I said okay.
7. *Savings and checking accounts* — Frank had already emptied them out.
8. *My car, valued at $3,000* — I asked Frank if I could have it. He said okay, but I had to take it out of his name immediately. I said okay.
9. *Truck, paid in full* — Frank wanted it. I said okay.
10. *$30,000 Frank inherited from his parents* — I didn't feel any of this was mine, so when Frank said he wanted it, I said okay.

As we were finishing up, Frank asked his attorney, "If we have any back taxes, shouldn't it be her responsibility to pay half the bill?"

Frank's attorney looked and him and said, "Frank, you're getting everything." I held my hand up and said that was okay. I would pay half.

I remember Frank laughing and patting me on the back, jokingly saying to his lawyer, "See how well we get along? Makes you wonder why we're getting a divorce."

I walked out with my car that was valued at about $3,000 and my wedding ring. I decided right then that I would someday give my wedding ring to my daughter, Connie.

A few weeks later, we went before the judge and were divorced. The first thing Frank said to me as we went out the door was that he wanted the car out of his name in case I wrecked it.

At the courthouse in Bath County, I found out I had to have insurance to put the car in my name. A friend of mine had a brother who owned an insurance company, and he faxed a binder to the courthouse so I could get the car in my name.

As we were walking out of the courthouse after changing the car title, Frank handed me a back tax bill he had gotten it in the mail. The bill was $489, and I needed to pay half. That was over half of my money for the next month. I said okay. This was wrong of Frank, but I also know this was part of him.

I was a divorced woman, forty-five years old. No one at work knew much about me. I stayed to myself. I always did my job. I made it a point to do much more than was expected of me.

One day when I was getting my mail at the main office, my supervisor walked past me. She asked, "Are you getting a divorce?" I was stunned. Why would she ask this? I hadn't talked to her since she interviewed me. She told me later she had not wanted to hire me because I seemed so quiet and nice, too easygoing to work with the most emotionally disturbed ten-year-old boys on campus.

I answered her question with a question. "Why do you ask?" She said she just wondered because I seemed to be on campus more than usual. I told her yes. She said it seemed like everyone was getting a divorce. Then she walked away, and I went back to my room to think.

I was so alone after my divorce. I was okay while the Re-Ed children were there, but they went home Friday at noon and did not return until Monday morning. I seemed to just walk from one room to the next. I had given up everything. I needed to begin building a place in the world where I could be me and have peace.

At Re-Ed, I changed positions from the boys group to the ten-year old girls group. I was working with a group counselor named Megan who was engaged to a man in Louisville. She went to Louisville every Friday and came back on Sunday.

She was saying she needed somewhere to stay during the week. She worked 1:30 till 9 PM Monday through Friday. Megan and I were sitting and talking, and I told her I wasn't getting any sleep. The girls in the groups I was working with were having problems at night, and during the day there were so many people coming and going in the cottage, it was hard to get any sleep.

Laura had walked in while we were talking. She said, "Why don't you go to my house during the day?" She said she was never there during the daytime. She told me she had rental property she managed during the mornings and her Re-Ed hours began at 1 PM. I was off work from 8 AM until 4 PM. I said that sounded good.

About an hour later, she came back to the cottage and said she had been thinking maybe I should stay with a friend of hers who lived in Chevy Chase. Her friend had a child who was in school during the day. I told her I didn't know where Chevy Chase was and Laura lived within walking distance. I remember thinking there was a chance she was trying to back out of her offer; she had always lived alone. Then I got busy with work and forgot all about it.

Chapter 21
ENDINGS AND BEGINNINGS

I needed some time to get strong. I lived in my mind when I was alone. I was still a child with Mary Jane, my make-believe mother. I was so happy in that world, not dealing with anything.

Some strange things were going on in my mind. I would drive and have to stop. I would be confused and could not remember where I was going. I would pull the car over to the side of the road and park. I remember thinking, *did I take the Re-Ed children to school this morning?* At times I felt like I was losing my mind. For the first time, I really felt like I was going crazy.

I knew I had to get help, so I went to counseling. My counselor went step-by-step through my life. As she did, I could feel myself accepting me more for who I was. She told me I needed to spend more time with my life and less time with my make-believe family. She wanted me to get to a place where I didn't need them anymore. I knew she was right, so I eventually did what she asked. My counselor suggested I leave them gracefully.

I thought about it for a long time. After over a year of counseling, the time came for me to leave my make-believe family. This was one of the hardest things I have ever done.

Re-Ed was going camping for a week, and I told everyone I couldn't go. It was summer. I went to my special place alone, a hillside with a little white house. Here was the spot I had picked for my make-believe family when I first moved to Bath County. There I thought about my make-believe family, and it was there my dad had a heart attack and died. We were all brokenhearted.

Mom was in her seventies. She cried herself to sleep and died during the night. My brothers just drifted away, living their lives in other places of the world. I cried the entire weekend. I was alone.

For the first time since I was a child, my make-believe family was gone. How I loved them. I could never explain how much they helped this little girl no one cared about. What a wonderful thing the mind can be. My heart was broken. There was such emptiness deep in my heart and I had to go through it alone. Before, at any point in my sad life, I could have drifted away and left reality and I would not have been alone, but now my security blanket was gone. But my resolve was strong, and I knew I would survive. I was an adult, I would be okay.

Laura and I had come to an arrangement where I would go to her house to sleep after I had taken my group of students to school every morning. She was usually gone, but I was talking more to her at work. We were becoming friends. She was so upfront with everything and always busy. No one could ask for a better supervisor. She would confront you if you didn't do your job and left you alone when you did your job well.

We started going shopping and fixing meals together. We did other things like looking for houses to buy. She was into buying houses, fixing them up, and making some money. I didn't have anything to do on weekends now, so I helped her with some of her projects.

Frank and I were still talking, and I called Keith every morning. I still sat in my room and did a lot of daydreaming.

One day, Mom called me. It was the first time I had heard from her in a long time. She said her husband was in the hospital and he was dying, but that wasn't why she called me. She told me my youngest half-brother had been arrested and there had been a trial. He was found guilty of sexually abusing an eight-year-old child. He was to be sentenced the next day. She wanted me to take her to Pomeroy, so I did.

The judge gave him one year without probation. Mom cried all the way home. He was her last child, the only child out of six that she spent much time with during his childhood.

When we got to Mom's house, there was a message on her phone saying her husband had died. I felt so sorry for her I decided I would take care of her again. I started going in every week and spending time with her. This is when I found out Mom was in big trouble with her bank. All of her money from social security was going to companies that got her personal information from her sweepstake entries. Money was being withdrawn from her checking account every month by these companies, and her checks for her utilities were bouncing.

Mom said I had to put the house back in my name immediately. When I asked why, she told me she had sent her deed to a man in Germany. He told her he needed the deed to her house, her social security card, and a blank check as proof that she was the winner of the million-dollar sweepstakes.

We went straight to the courthouse and found out there was not a lien on her house, went to the bank and closed her account, and then went to a lawyer and had him put the house in my name, giving her a lifetime estate so she would always have a place to live.

After I got everything worked out, Mom started giving me a hard time. She said that since the house now belonged to me, I needed to do some upkeep on it. There were some repairs needed.

I redid the floor and the walls in the kitchen. I put ceiling fans in the kitchen, living room, and her bedroom. I had the front porch screened in so the mosquitoes wouldn't bother her. I had her bathroom completely renovated so it was handicapped accessible and everything was more convenient for her.

I had to take a loan for all of these repairs and improvements to the home. I also had to get insurance on the house since Mom had refused to pay insurance while it was in her name.

For the next few weeks, Mom kept coming up with statements like, "You don't need this house; you're the richest of all my children." One day, she called me, and her first words were, "I want my house back. You don't need it. Why should you have my house when I've mowed this yard and paid all the telephone bills for years?"

All I said was no. This is when she said, "You are nobody to me. Give me my house back. I hate you, you Donahue bitch. Your youngest brother called me, and he's having a hard time. I want him to have this house."

I decided to pay my mother a visit and try to talk to her. She stood on her screened-in porch with the door locked. That was the last time I saw my mother.

I've gotten letters from her saying she wants her house back, letters telling me how much she hates me, phone calls telling me she wished I were dead. Why was my heart broken again? Why do I hurt so much inside? Why do I love my mother the way I do? All these questions kept resurfacing.

This last round with my mother took everything out of me and left me weak. I felt so empty. I knew my lifetime dream would never come true, and funny as this may sound, I no longer wanted it to come true.

I believed with all my heart that my mother was gone from me forever this time, as if she had suddenly died. I felt relief, after the grief. I would never have to see the hate in her eyes or hear the devastating words again. My mother was gone forever.

This is when I began writing my story, and now I'm coming to the end. I still do not understand. I may never understand. I still want her to call me and say she's sorry and that she loves me. I know this will never happen, and if it does, it will be because she wants or needs something again from me.

So deep down inside, I pray, dear God, please don't let her call me. I can't go through this rejection again.

I have come to the conclusion that all of my mother's children were nobodies to her. I know this because I am the one who kept returning, always trying to win her love—a love that she is incapable of giving.

So now I come to the end of my writing. When I started, I was sixty-four years old and now I am sixty-five.

I just looked up, and my dearest friend and companion just walked in. She looked over at me and asked if I was cold. I shook my head no. Yes, she is my guardian angel now. It's strange how much she is like Barbara, with her strong voice and her quick mind.

Any time I venture too far in the wrong direction or get too close to danger, she grabs my hand and quickly pulls me back, back to where I'm safe. I can be me at all times. I feel so safe and loved.

I have been with Laura over twenty years, and she has become my true soul mate. I can't put into words how much I love and trust her. She is the only one I have ever told about my make-believe family.

She seems to know all my strange behaviors—like jumping when she walks in quickly, or my fear of the unknown. She doesn't know why, but that doesn't seem to matter. She just takes over when I need to be by myself or

I need time to get back together again. I have had only one person like this come along in my lifetime. For the first time, I know I am going to be okay.

Barbara, Frank, and Laura were like a tag team, taking over and completing a section of my life. Frank was my hardest. I had so much to accomplish as a young woman, wife, and mother. Also complicating matters was my sexual side, which was so damaged.

It was easier for me with Barbara and Laura because they were women, and some of the parts of me that were so damaged could be sealed and put away. These could not be sealed and put away in married life.

At the beginning of this writing, I have said good-bye to my mother for the last time. What sadness I have when I think of her. I know I will not go to her funeral; this would serve no purpose, and I have already said good-bye.

I'm ending this with a tear in my eyes because I still love her and I cannot stand the thought of her being alone or hurt. I know I would not be the one she would want holding her hand in the end. She would want a male friend or maybe a son. What a strange obsession my mother had with men.

I sit here now looking at all these pages, court records, and pictures. I'm finished writing my story, but what do I do with all these memories and nightmares I've uncovered? All my bad dreams are back, just when I had finally gotten to the point where I was rarely having them. These dreams were some of the scariest parts of my life. I hated the dark because that is where the most evil people hide, and the dark is when the dreams came. Night is when we are supposed to sleep. I couldn't. I could finally sleep when the sun peeked through the sky. Only then could I be comforted by my warm, soft bed and sleep like a baby.

Recalling my past, I'm having trouble sleeping again. I want to be alone. I cry easily. I jump when I hear a noise. I have become frightened once again when someone enters my room quickly or unannounced.

Years have passed since I went into that dark hole in my mind, the place where I stored all of my sadness, hurtfulness, and shame of who I was.

Why, after all this time, did I think that by unlocking the past and writing about it I would have a better understanding? Right now, I can't answer that question.

I do know that I have to put myself back together, just like I was able to do under my porch long ago. I can do this just as before. I will be Mary Jane's and Clell's "Little Erma." I will be happy and enjoy the rest of my life. I know it won't be easy, but I will do it one stick at a time.

Doc.# 3a.

1-50-25   THE COLUMBUS BLANK BOOK MFG. CO., COL., O.   3758

COMPLAINT
AS TO DELINQUENT, NEGLECTED, DEPENDENT OR CRIPPLED CHILD
Gen'l Code. Secs. 1639-23 11432-16

Juvenile Court, *Meigs* County, Ohio

IN THE MATTER OF
Erma Jane, Freddie, & Jimmy Older

a dependent & neglected children

The undersigned says that he has knowledge of

Oct. 8, '45; Aug. 3, '49;

a minor under the age of 18 *years, to-wit, the age of* 7, 3; & 1 Apr. 7, 52

years; that said minor appears to be a dependent & neglected children

in this: that they lack proper parental care by reason of faults & habits of their parents; their conditions are such as to warrant the state, in the interests of the children in assuming their guardianship.

Said minor is not an inmate of a state institution, or any institution incorporated under the laws of the State for the care and correction of delinquent, neglected and dependent children.

The name of the person having custody or control of said minor, or with whom they are now is, is William Older & Agnes Older

and resides at East Letart, Ohio

That the of said child resides at

Robert Stein

The State of Ohio, Meigs *County, ss.*

The undersigned being duly sworn says that the statements in the foregoing complaint are true as he verily believes.

Robert Stein

Sworn to before me and signed in my presence this 2nd *day of* January 1953

F. H. O'Brien

139

Doc. # 3b.

12-46-E   THE COLUMBUS BLANK BOOK MFG. CO., COL. O.   3895

AFFIDAVIT

Charging Non-Support

Gen'l Code, Secs. 1639-46, 13432-1, -5, -9, -12

The State of Ohio, _Meigs_ _____ County, ss.   JUVENILE COURT

Before me, _F. H. O'Brien_ _____, Judge of the Juvenile Court
of said County, personally came _Robert Stivers_ _____
who, being duly sworn according to law deposes and says that on or about the
_2nd_ day of _January_ _____, 19_53_ at the County of _Meigs_ _____
aforesaid, and from the _1st_ day of _December_ _____, 19_52_ until the said
_2nd_ day of _January_ _____, 19_53_, one _William Older_ _____
being then and there the ¹ _father_ _____, and charged by law with
the care, support, maintenance and education of one _Erma Jane, Freddie_
+ Jimmy Older _____
a minor under the age of eighteen years, to-wit, of the age of _7, 3, 2/3 yrs. resp_
years, and being able to contribute towards the care, support, maintenance and education of the said _minor children_ _____ willfully and unlawfully did, then
and there ² _fail to ³ support and educate_
the said minor ___ he, the said _William Older_ well knowing the said _children_
_____ to be such minor,⁴ contrary to the General Code in such case
made and provided, and against the peace and dignity of the State of Ohio.

Robert Stivers

Sworn to and subscribed before me, this _2nd_ day of _January_ _____ 19_53_

F. H. O'Brien
Judge of said Juvenile Court

_____
Deputy Clerk

140

Doc. # 3c.

ENDORSEMENT
Gen'l Code, Secs. 1639-24

The State of Ohio, *Meigs* County, ss. JUVENILE COURT

To *Robert Stivers* Probation Officer—~~Sheriff~~ of said County, Greeting:

It appears that said child *you is in* such conditions or surroundings that *their*
welfare requires the Court to assume immediate custody.

You are, therefore, hereby directed to take said child *into* custody at once and
make due return of this citation with endorsements.

WITNESS my signature and the Seal of said Court
this *2nd* day of *January* 19*53*

F. H. O'Brien
Juvenile Judge

BA
Deputy Clerk

RETURN

Office of *Juvenile Court*

Meigs County, Ohio

January 2nd 19*53*

Received this writ *January 2nd* 19*53*, at *1* o'clock *P* M.
and on the *2nd* day of *January* 19*53*, I served the same by
delivering a true copy thereof personally to the within named *William*
Older & Agnes Older

SHERIFF'S FEES	
Service and Return	$
Mileage _____ miles, per mile 8c	
Total	

Robert Stivers
Probation Officer—~~Sheriff~~

9-45-1   THE COLUMBUS BLANK BOOK MFG. CO., COL., O.   Doc. #3d.

CITATION

(Copy to Serve)

To Minor and to Person Having Custody or Control of Minor, or with Whom Minor May Be.

Gen'l Code, Secs. 1639-24, 3615

The State of Ohio, *Meigs* _____ County, ss.   JUVENILE COURT

To *Robert Stivers* _____ Probation Officer—~~Sheriff~~ of said County, Greeting:

You are hereby directed to cite *Erma Jane, Freddie, & Jimmy Older* *minors* and *William Older & Agnes Older* the person having custody or control of the child or with whom they may be, to appear with said minors before the Judge of the Juvenile Court of said County, at the Court House in *Pomeroy* _____, on the *5th* day of *January*, 19*53* at *10* o'clock *A*.M., and to abide the order of the Judge. The affidavit filed in said Court sets forth that said Minors appears to be *dependent & neglected* in this; that *they lack proper parental care by reason of faults & habits of their parents; their conditions are such as to warrant the state, in the interests of the children, in assuming their guardian ship*

The person so cited failing to appear may be punished as in other cases for contempt of Court.

You will make due return of this citation on the *2nd* _____ day of *January* 19 *53*

WITNESS my signature and the seal of said Court this *2nd* day of *January*, 19*53*

[SEAL]

J. H. O'Brien
Judge of said Juvenile Court

By *Robt Stivers*
Deputy Clerk

1. "Dependent," "Neglected," "Delinquent."

5-43-2   THE COLUMBUS BLANK BOOK MFG. CO., COL., O.   3756

CITATION

To minor and to person having custody or control of it, or with whom it may be.

Gen'l Code, Secs. 1639-24, 3038

The State of Ohio, *Meigs* County, ss.   JUVENILE COURT

To *Robert Stivers* Probation Officer—~~Sheriff~~ of said County, Greeting:

You are hereby directed to cite *Erma Jane, Freddie, & Jimmy Older*
a minor, and *William Older & Agnes Older*
the persons having custody or control of the child or with whom it may be, to appear
with said minors before the Judge of the Juvenile Court of said County at the Court
House in *Pomeroy*, on the *5th* day of *January* 1953,
at *10* o'clock *A.* M., and to abide the order of the Judge. The affidavit filed in
said Court sets forth that said minors appears to be *dependent & neglected*
in this; that *they lack proper parental care by reason*
of faults and habits of their parents;
their conditions are such as to warrant the
state, in the interests of the children, in
assuming their guardianship.

The person so cited failing to appear may be punished as in other cases for contempt
of court.

You will make due return of this citation on the *2nd* day of

143

Doc.#3f.

RETURN
Gen'l Code, Secs. 2834, 2836, 3038.

_Pomeroy_____, Ohio, _January 2nd_____, 19_53_

Received this Writ on the _2ud_ day of _January_____, 19_53_, at

_10_ o'clock _A_ _M_., and pursuant to its command I forthwith on the _2nd_

day of _January_____, 19_53_, executed it by taking the within named

_William Older_____ *and delivering to h_im_ a copy

thereof, including a copy of the affidavit filed upon which said Writ was issued:

and now have h_is_ body before the Court.

SHERIFF'S FEES	
Service and Return,____ Persons each $1.00 $ ____	
Mileage,____ miles at 8c · · · · ____	
____	
____	
Total · · · · · · $ ____	

Robert Stiveis

Probation Officer—~~Sheriff~~

Assistant—Deputy

* If no copy is delivered these two lines should be omitted, (effaced).

Doc. #3g.

Erma Jane (Backus? Morgan?) Older – 10/8/4
Freddie Older – 8/3/49
Jimmy " – 4/7/52.

W^m. & Agnes Older claim to have to
married at White Oak, Ky. "about
5 years ago". Have no paper of any
kind, as proof.

"Mr. O. was divorced in Columbus
"about 5½ yrs. ago"; no children
by first marriage. Former address
was 3661 Plainview Drive

W^m. has been working for Clyde
Norris, Howard Norris, Roy Pearson,
Pete Shields, Dale Hill. Gets $2.50
per day; claims to work "almost
every day".

Just moved into 4-room shack,
windows out, wind blows through;
many cracks; has stove, table, &
refrigerator in kitchen; bed, dresser, &
chairs in one; another b.r., & bed &
dresser; bedclothes very dirty, as
was whole house, & clothing. Carry
water from well on hill 108 ft.

145

Doc #3h.

I 40.1   THE COLUMBUS BLANK BOOK MFG. CO., COL., O.   3812

WARRANT TO ARREST
ON AFFIDAVIT CHARGING NON-SUPPORT.
Gen'l. Code, Secs. 1639-46, 52, 53, 13432-4 to 13-19.

The State of Ohio, _Meigs_____ County, ss.

To _Robert Stivers_____ Probation Officer—Sheriff of said County, Greeting:
     Whereas, there has been filed with me an affidavit of which the following is a copy:

The State of Ohio, _Meigs_____ County, ss.   JUVENILE COURT

     Before me, _F. H. O'Brien_____, Judge of the Juvenile Court
of said County, personally came _Robert Stivers_____
who, being duly sworn according to law, deposes and says that on or about the _2nd_
day of _January_____ 19_53_ at the County of _Meigs_____ aforesaid, and
from the _1st_ day of _December_, 19_52_ until the said _2nd_ day of
January, 19_53_ one _William Older_____
being then and there the _father_____, and charged by law
with the care, support, maintenance and education of one _Erma Jane, Freddie, &_
_Jimmy Older_____ minors under the age of eighteen years, to-wit, of the age
of _7, 3 & 2½ resp_ years, and being able to contribute toward the care, support, maintenance and education of the said _Erma Jane, Freddie & Jimmy Older_
willfully and unlawfully did, then and there _fail to support and to_
_educate_____ the said minors he, the said
_William Older_____ well knowing the said _Erma Jane, Freddie, &_
_Jimmy Older_____ to be such minors

         _Robert Stivers_____

Sworn to and subscribed before me, this _2nd_ day of _January_____ 19_53_

         _F. H. O'Brien_____
         Judge of said Juvenile Court

         Deputy Clerk
     These are therefore to command you to take the said
_William Older_____ if he be found in your County, or, if he
is not found in your County, that you pursue after him in any other County in this
State, and take and safely keep the said _William Older_____
so that you have his body forthwith before me to answer the said complaint, and be
further dealt with according to law.

Doc.# 4a.

THE COLUMBUS BLANK BOOK MFG. CO., COL., O.   3784

COMPLAINT
AS TO DELINQUENT, NEGLECTED, DEPENDENT OR CRIPPLED CHILD
Rev. Code, Secs 2151 21, 2995 19

Juvenile Court, _____ Meigs _____ County, Ohio

IN THE MATTER OF

Erma Older, Fred Older, James
Older, Jeanie Older, Bobby Older

No. *17246*

a ¹ _____ neglected _____ *child* ren

The undersigned says that_____ he has knowledge of

Erma Older, Fred Older, James Older, Jeanie Older, Bobby Older

a minor under the age of ² eighteen *years, to-wit, the age of* 10, 6, 4, 2, *years*
and 3 months, respectively,
that said minor appears to be a ¹ _____ neglected _____ *child* re

in this: that they lack proper parental care because of the faults

or habits of their parents.

Said minor is not an inmate of a state institution, or any institution incorporated under the laws of the State for the care and correction of delinquent, neglected and dependent children.

The name of the person having custody or control of said minor, or with whom

it now is, is William Older and Agnes Older,

and resides at _____ Letart, Ohio,

That _____ *the* ³ _____ parents _____ *of said child* re

resides at ⁴ Letart, Ohio, being William and Agnes Older,

Carl Gorby

The State of Ohio, _____ Meigs _____ County, ss.

The undersigned being duly sworn says that the statements in the foregoing complaint are true as __ he verily believes.

Carl Gorby

Sworn to before me and signed in my presence this _____ 3rd _____ *day of*

_____ May, _____ 19 56.

John G. Bacon

147

Doc. # 4b

COLUMBUS BLANK BOOK CO., COL., O. 3758

CITATION

To Parents, Guardian or the Person having custody or control of the child, or with whom
such child may be.

Rev. Code, Secs. 2151.28, .29

17246

The State of Ohio, __Meigs__ County, ss. JUVENILE COURT

To __Carl Gorby,__ Probation Officer—~~Sheriff of said County~~ Greeting:

You are hereby directed to cite William Older, Agnes Older, Erma Older,
Fred Older, James Older, Jennie Older, Bobby Older,

the parents being William Older and Agnes Older, *, to personally be*
and appear with the five last named being *, the Child* ren *named in the*
Complaint, before the Judge of the Juvenile Court of said County at the Court House
in Pomeroy, Ohio, *on the* 10th *day of* May, *1956*
at 10:00 *o'clock* A.M. *and to abide the order of the Court. The Complaint*
filed in said Court sets forth that said Children appear *to be* neglected
in this: they lack proper parental care because of the faults or
habits of their parents,

The person so cited failing to appear may be punished as in other cases for contempt
of court.

You will make due return of this citation on the 7th *day of*
May, *19*56

WITNESS my signature and the seal of said Court,
this 3rd *day of* May, *19*56

John C. Bacon
Judge of the Juvenile Court

By *Martha Jane Williams*
Deputy Clerk

Doc.#4c

COLUMBUS BLANK BOOK CO., COL., O.   3757

JOURNAL ENTRY—Order for Citation
Rev. Code. Sec. 2151-28

Juvenile Court,   Meigs   County, Ohio

May 3rd   1956

In the Matter of   / 7 2 46
Erma Older, et al   *an alleged*   neglected   *minor*

This day Carl Gorby, Probation Officer,   *filed with the Judge of this*
Court an affidavit setting forth that Erma, F_ed, James, Jeanie, Bobby Older
a minor under the age of eighteen years, appears to be neglected. it appears
they are in such surroundings that their welfare requires the Court to
~~xxxxxxxxxxxxxxxxxxxxxxxxxxxxxxxxxxxxxxxx~~
assume immediate custody. It is ordered that a citation issue requiring
William Older and Agnes Older. *the parents, guardian or the persons hav-*
ing custody or control of the child or with whom such child may be, to appear person-
ally and bring the said minor before the Judge of this Court, on the 10th *day*
of May, , 19 56, *at* 9:00 *o'clock* A.M., *and this cause is*
continued, the children to be taken into immediate custody.

John C Bacon
Judge

1. Dependent, Neglected or Delinquent.

149

Doc. # 4d.

ENDORSEMENT

Rev. Code. Sec. 2151.26

The State of Ohio,   Meigs   County, ss.   JUVENILE COURT

To   Carl Gorby,   Probation Officer—Sheriff of said County, Greeting:

It appears that said child ren is in such conditions or surroundings that welfare requires the Court to assume immediate custody.

You are, therefore, hereby directed to take said child ren into custody at once and make due return of this citation with endorsements.

WITNESS my signature and the Seal of said Court this 3rd day of May , 19 56

John C. Bacon

Juvenile Judge

By

Deputy Clerk

RETURN

Office of   Juvenile Court

Meigs   County, Ohio

May 3,   1956

Received this writ   May 3,   19 56 , at   2   o'clock   P. M.

and on the   3rd day of   May   1956 , I served the same by

* delivering a true copy thereof to   the within named

William and Agnes Older

SHERIFF'S FEES
Service and Return - - - - - - - - - $
Mileage   miles per mile 6c
Total - - - - - -

Carl Gorby

Probation Officer—Sheriff

* delivering a true copy thereof personally to' or, 'leaving a true copy thereof at the usual place of residence of

150

Doc. # 4d.

ENDORSEMENT
Rev. Code, Sec. 2151.28

The State of Ohio, _____ Meigs _____ County, ss.   JUVENILE COURT

To _____ Carl Gorby, _____ Probation Officer—Sheriff of said County, Greeting:

It appears that said child ren is in such conditions or surroundings that _____ welfare requires the Court to assume immediate custody.

You are, therefore, hereby directed to take said child ren into custody at once and make due return of this citation with endorsements.

WITNESS my signature and the Seal of said Court this 3rd *day of* May , 19 56

John C. Bacon

Juvenile Judge

By _____

Deputy Clerk

RETURN

Office of _____ Juvenile Court _____

_____ Meigs _____ County, Ohio

May 3, _____ 1956

Received this writ _____ May 3, _____ 19 56 , *at* 2 *o'clock* P M.

and on the 3rd *day of* May _____ 1956 , *I served the same by* * delivering a true copy thereof to _____ *the within named* _____ William and Agnes Older

SHERIFF'S FEES	
Service and Return . . . . $ _____	
Mileage _____ miles per mile 8c . . .	
	Carl Gorby
	Probation Officer Sheriff
Total	

* "delivering a true copy thereof personally to" or, "leaving a true copy thereof at the usual place of residence of".

Doc.#4e.

IN THE JUVENILE COURT OF MEIGS COUNTY, OHIO

In the matter of

Erma Older, Fred Older,
James Older, Jeanie Older,
Bobby Older,

neglected children

No. 17,246

JOURNAL ENTRY

This day this cause came on to be heard upon the complaint and the evidence, William Older and Agnes Older, being in Court and the children's presence being excused, present also being Carl Gorby, probation officer, and

The Court upon the evidence finds Erma Older, Fred Older, James Older, Jeanie Older and Bobby Older, minors under eighteen years of age, to be neglected children in this: they lack proper parental care because of the faults or habits of their parents, William Older and Agnes Older, and therefore come into the custody of the Court, and will continue for all necessary purposes of discipline and protection, a ward of the Court, until they become 21 years of age.

It is further ordered and adjudged that the said Erma Older, Fred Older, James Older, Jeanie Older and Bobby Older, be committed to the permanent care and custody of the Meigs County Child Welfare Board with permission and power to place said children in a foster home with the probability of adoption, and this cause is continued for any and all further orders that may be necessary.

John Bacon
Juvenile Judge

COLUMBUS BLANK BOOK CO., COL., O.   Doc. 4 4f.   3757

JOURNAL ENTRY—Order for Citation
Rev. Code. Sec 2151.28

Juvenile Court,   Meigs   County, Ohio

May 3rd   1956
                                    /7246
In the Matter of   *an alleged*   neglected   *minor*
    Erma Older, et al

                                                        filed with the Judge of this
This day Carl Corby, Probation Officer,

Court an affidavit setting forth that Erma, Fred, James, Jeenie, Bobby Older.

a minor under the age of eighteen years, appears to be   neglected, it appears
they are in such surroundings that their welfare requires the Court to
~~per~~~~xxxxxxxxxxxxxxxxxxxxxxxxxxxxx~~ It is ordered that a citation issue requiring
~~a~~ume immediate custody,
    William Older and Agnes Older.   *the parents, guardian or the persons hav-*

ing custody or control of the child or with whom such child may be, to appear person-

ally and bring the said minor before the Judge of this Court, on the 10th *day*

of May, *19 56, at* 9:00 *o'clock* A.M., *and this cause is*

continued, the children to be taken into immediate custody.

                                    John Bacon
                                                              Judge

1. Dependent, Neglected or Delinquent.

Neighbor reports that Older child came to her home on Sunday evening asking for
help for her little brother. Little girl said her Mother had been gone from home since
Friday afternoon. Neighbor came with Erma to the home and found unbelievable horrible
conditions where the children were living. The neighbor reported she believed the baby
was dying. She returned home and called the police, ambulance and social services was
notified. Neighbor returned to the Older home with water, clean clothes and began trying
to lower the baby's temperature. She states the baby had harden feces all over his back
and sores that look infected from feces. The neighbor gave her statement then returned
to her home. She appeared visibly shaken by her discovery.
    Living conditions noted by authorities; one room shack with extended small space
about 3 ft. in height. Chicken wire covered by some boards. appears to have been a
chicken coop, looks like children slept in this small area.
    No electric, no heat, no water, no milk and no food are present. Furniture consists of
1 bed, apparently for the adults. No sheets, blankets or pillows in home. One small table
with 2 chairs. Table has flies and maggots on surface with decayed food. Also on table
are beer bottles, cigarette butts, matches, a bottle of ink and needles. A small heating
stove with a pot on top of stove with what appears to be a chicken, half eaten. Feathers
are still on the chicken and all over the floor. There appears to be cow feed all over the
home. Clothes are on the floor. Everything is filthy.

Doc. #4g.

COLUMBUS BLANK BOOK CO., COL., O.   3767

JOURNAL ENTRY—Order for Citation
Rev. Code. Sec. 2151.28

Juvenile Court, _____Meigs_____ County, Ohio

May 3rd _____ 19 56

In the Matter of
  Erma Older, et al   *an alleged* _17246_
                                                   neglected _____ minor³

This day Carl Gorby, Probation Officer, _____ *filed with the Judge of this*
Court an affidavit setting forth that Erma, Fred, James, Jeanie, Bobby Older
a minor under the age of eighteen years, appears to be ¹ neglected, it appears
they are in such surroundings that their welfare requires the Court to
~~pxxxxxxxxxxxxxxxxxxxxxxxxxxxxxxxxxxxxxxx~~
sume immediate custody, It is ordered that a citation issue requiring
William Older and Agnas Older. *the parents, guardian or the persons hav-*
ing custody or control of the child or with whom such child may be, to appear person-
ally and bring the said minor before the Judge of this Court, on the 10th *day*
of May, _____, 19 56, *at* 9:00 *o'clock* A.M., *and this cause is*
continued, the children to be taken into immediate custody.

_____ *Judge*

1. Dependent, Neglected or Delinquent.

Condition of Older children;
   Erma; left arm appears infected from homemade tattoo, bruises visible on arms, legs.
Appears to have the role of caretaker of her sister and brothers.
   Freddie; pronounced speech impairment, almost impossible to understand what he
saying. Bruises appear to be all over his body. He is angry, hostile and scared. Appears
protective of siblings.
 * Note Father states he can't do anything with him.
   James; quiet, frighten, bruises all over, watches Erma for instructions.
   Jeannie; sits in corner, quiet, mouth busted, appears to be misshapen, can't stand or
walk, can't sit with back straight, has almost no hair, diaper pins rusted to her skin,
appears emaciated. Sent to hospital by car.
   Bobby; also appears emaciated, appears unconscious, taken to hospital by ambulance.

6

Ohio Penitentiary

Ohio Penitentiary at Columbus Sketch
Contributor: Ohio Historical Society

These are the prisons Mom & Bill spent time in.

Short term sentences of weeks or months were served in the county jails.

The Ohio Penitentiary opened in Columbus in 1834 and continued to house prisoners until 1979. The state had built a small prison in Columbus in 1813. But as the state's population grew the earlier facility was not able to handle the number of prisoners sent to it by the courts. When the penitentiary first opened in 1834, not all of the buildings were completed.

A separate facility for women prisoners was completed within the walls of the Ohio Penitentiary in 1837. A number of women served on death row in the prison and ultimately faced execution either by hanging or in the electric chair. A separate prison called the Ohio Reformatory for Women was completed in 1913 in Marysville and the last women left the Ohio Penitentiary.

(Above Left) *Me and my husband in our first year of marriage.*
(Above Right) *Me*
(Lower Left) *Me and my husband attending a wedding.*
(Lower Right) Me & Mom at Connie's wedding.

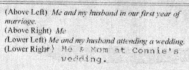

(Top Left) *Me when I was pregnant with my first child.*
(Bottom Left)- *Me with my second child.*
(Below) *Me and my husband at a Church*

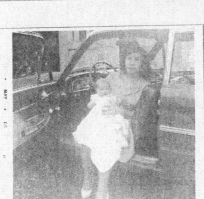

Beech Grove Cemetery Across The Road from Children's Home- *I would run away from the Children's Home to this Cemetery where Barbara would find me.*

Beech Grove Cemetery – *I always slept behind this tombstone since it was the biggest at the time.*

Epilogue

All through my book, I talk about how strong I think I am, but I know that I have been on the brink of living in a mental institution, never talking, never having any responsibility, and just living in my mind. Sometimes I think what a wonderful way to live it is, to imagine, having only good things happen.

Well, that's my life, or what I remember from the beginning until now. I know I left out some happy memories and many more sad ones. I went all these years never saying anything about my childhood or my mom's abuse toward me—me with all my secrets. When my children went to my mother's house, she was always pleasant but a little distant. I remember my daughter saying she didn't think her grandmother really wanted them there. I didn't tell her, but she was absolutely right. Mom didn't want anyone around her she couldn't benefit from.

I remember a show that came on TV when Frank and I first married. The show was called *Naked City*. This was in the sixties. They always ended with, "There are 8 million stories in the Naked City, and you have just heard one." Well, there are probably 8 million abused children, and I am just one of them.

Acknowledgments

I would like to thank the Meigs County Library staff. A special thanks to the Meigs County Sheriff's Office and especially to Sheriff Bob Beagle. Thanks to Edie Luce for all of her hard work, the research on children's homes, and especially for being such a kind, caring person to everyone. Barbara Stout, how do you say thanks to a person who held my hand all through my childhood? She was the only person that told me she loved me and showed it. This book would not have been possible without the invaluable assistance of Susie Donahue. She researched, traveled, and held my hand from beginning to end. A special thanks to my daughter, Connie, for all her hard work, love, and understanding. She gathered photos, gave advice, and also worked on the book cover. Many thanks to my son, Keith Steppe. He helped me put it all together in the end. My true soul mate and companion, Laura, has stood by me this last year. She has endured my nightmares, my irritability, my inability to stop crying at times, and she is still here.

My true soul mate and companion, Laura, has stood by me this last year. She has withstood my nightmares, my irritability, my inability to stop crying at times and she is still here.

Manufactured By: RR Donnelley
                    Breinigsville, PA USA
                    February, 2011